STUDENT MANUAL

Microsoft® Visio®
2013: Part 2

Microsoft® Visio®
2013: Part 2

Microsoft® Visio® 2013: Part 2

Part Number: 091115
Course Edition: 1.0

Acknowledgements

PROJECT TEAM

Content Developer	Media Designer	Content Editor
John Bradley	Alex Tong	Catherine M. Albano

Notices

DISCLAIMER

TRADEMARK NOTICES

Microsoft® Visio® 2013: Part 2

About This Course

Microsoft® Visio® stands out among similar applications because of its unique ability to draw a wide variety of diagrams, flowcharts, workflows, and organization structures—anything that can be represented by shapes connected by lines. Most importantly, these shapes can be rearranged and with corresponding lines remaining intact. Visio has improved over the years as features common among Microsoft® Office applications have been added. Today, Visio is well integrated with other members of the Office family as well as Microsoft's cloud-based services. This greatly enriches the sharing and publishing of Visio drawings.

Microsoft® Visio® 2013 : Part 1, you learned the basic skills needed to create and modify various Visio drawings. *Microsoft® Visio® 2013 : Part 2*, you will learn about more advanced features—making you a more efficient and effective Visio user.

Course Description

Target Student

The target student for this course is a graphic designer, subject matter specialist, or other knowledge worker with basic Microsoft Visio 2013 skills (such as creating basic workflows and other diagrams) who needs to use Visio to create complex graphics and illustrations (such as floor plans, custom maps, and scientific illustrations) that may be linked to external data sources and may be inserted into other Microsoft Office files.

Course Prerequisites

To ensure your success in this course, you should have the ability to create basic workflows and other common diagram types in Visio. You can obtain this level of knowledge and skills by taking the following Logical Operations course: *Microsoft® Visio® 2013: Part 1*.

Course Objectives

In this course, you will examine advanced features to make you more efficient and effective. You will:

- Enhance the look of drawings.
- Create shapes, stencils, and templates.
- Connect drawings to external data.
- Leverage development tools.
- Share drawings.
- Use diagram standards (optional).

http://www.lo-choice.com

The LogicalCHOICE Home Screen

The LogicalCHOICE Home screen is your entry point to the LogicalCHOICE learning experience, of which this course manual is only one part. Visit the LogicalCHOICE Course screen both during and after class to make use of the world of support and instructional resources that make up the LogicalCHOICE experience.

Log-on and access information for your LogicalCHOICE environment will be provided with your class experience. On the LogicalCHOICE Home screen, you can access the LogicalCHOICE Course screens for your specific courses.

Each LogicalCHOICE Course screen will give you access to the following resources:

- eBook: an interactive electronic version of the printed book for your course.
- LearnTOs: brief animated components that enhance and extend the classroom learning experience.

Depending on the nature of your course and the choices of your learning provider, the LogicalCHOICE Course screen may also include access to elements such as:

- The interactive eBook.
- Social media resources that enable you to collaborate with others in the learning community using professional communications sites such as LinkedIn or microblogging tools such as Twitter.
- Checklists with useful post-class reference information.
- Any course files you will download.
- The course assessment.
- Notices from the LogicalCHOICE administrator.
- Virtual labs, for remote access to the technical environment for your course.
- Your personal whiteboard for sketches and notes.
- Newsletters and other communications from your learning provider.
- Mentoring services.
- A link to the website of your training provider.
- The LogicalCHOICE store.

Visit your LogicalCHOICE Home screen often to connect, communicate, and extend your learning experience!

How to Use This Book

As You Learn

This book is divided into lessons and topics, covering a subject or a set of related subjects. In most cases, lessons are arranged in order of increasing proficiency.

The results-oriented topics include relevant and supporting information you need to master the content. Each topic has various types of activities designed to enable you to practice the guidelines and procedures as well as to solidify your understanding of the informational material presented in the course. Procedures and guidelines are presented in a concise fashion along with activities and discussions. Information is provided for reference and reflection in such a way as to facilitate understanding and practice.

Data files for various activities as well as other supporting files for the course are available by download from the LogicalCHOICE Course screen. In addition to sample data for the course exercises, the course files may contain media components to enhance your learning and additional reference materials for use both during and after the course.

At the back of the book, you will find a glossary of the definitions of the terms and concepts used throughout the course. You will also find an index to assist in locating information within the instructional components of the book.

As You Review

Any method of instruction is only as effective as the time and effort you, the student, are willing to invest in it. In addition, some of the information that you learn in class may not be important to you immediately, but it may become important later. For this reason, we encourage you to spend some time reviewing the content of the course after your time in the classroom.

As a Reference

The organization and layout of this book make it an easy-to-use resource for future reference. Taking advantage of the glossary, index, and table of contents, you can use this book as a first source of definitions, background information, and summaries.

Course Icons

Watch throughout the material for these visual cues:

Icon	Description
	A **Note** provides additional information, guidance, or hints about a topic or task.
	A **Caution** helps make you aware of places where you need to be particularly careful with your actions, settings, or decisions so that you can be sure to get the desired results of an activity or task.
	LearnTO notes show you where an associated LearnTO is particularly relevant to the content. Access LearnTOs from your LogicalCHOICE Course screen.
	Checklists provide job aids you can use after class as a reference to performing skills back on the job. Access checklists from your LogicalCHOICE Course screen.
	Social notes remind you to check your LogicalCHOICE Course screen for opportunities to interact with the LogicalCHOICE community using social media.
	Notes Pages are intentionally left blank for you to write on.

1 | Enhancing the Look of Drawings

Lesson Time: 1 hour, 30 minutes

Lesson Objectives

In this lesson, you will enhance the look of drawings. You will:

- Create a Microsoft account and log in to Visio.

- Change the look of shapes.

- Manipulate three-dimensional shapes.

- Apply backgrounds, borders, and titles to drawings.

- Define a style.

Lesson Introduction

When you're creating a drawing, your first priority should be a clear and accurate content. Your second priority should be visual appeal. If your drawing isn't attractive, it probably won't be used by the target audience. You don't have to be a graphic artist to produce a visually compelling piece. Visio® contains many tools that enable you to look like a pro even if you aren't.

TOPIC A

Create a Microsoft Account and Sign in to Visio

Before you start using Visio®, you need to know about Microsoft® accounts and how to use them with Visio. Signing in to Visio with a Microsoft account enables you take advantage of a number of important features.

Microsoft Accounts

A Microsoft account is an email address and password that you can use to sign into Microsoft products (such as Windows 8 and Office 2013) and services (such as OneDrive® and Outlook.com). You can create a Microsoft account by using an existing email address or you can create a new email address to use as your Microsoft account. Microsoft allows you to choose outlook.com, hotmail.com, or live.com as the domain for your new email address.

 Note: It's best to choose the outlook.com option—which is Microsoft's newest brand of web-based email service. The other two domains are legacy brands that Microsoft is slowly phasing out.

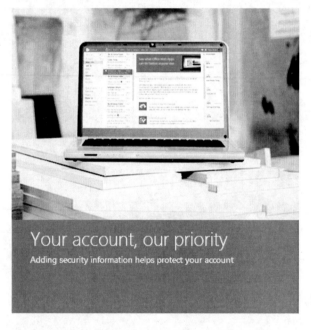
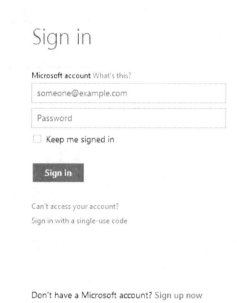

Figure 1-1: Signing in to a Microsoft account.

 Note: Visit **http://www.microsoft.com/en-us/account/default.aspx** to learn more about Microsoft accounts.

Microsoft Accounts and Visio

Whenever you use Visio, make sure you are signed in to the product with your Microsoft account. This enables you to access Visio templates and your drawings online. Whenever you sign in to Visio with your Microsoft account, Visio automatically connects to your OneDrive account.

The top right corner of Visio shows which Microsoft account is signed in currently. If the current account isn't yours, you can switch to your account.

Figure 1-2: Visio signed into a Microsoft account.

 Access the Checklist tile on your LogicalCHOICE course screen for reference information and job aids on How to Create a Microsoft Account and Sign in to Visio.

ACTIVITY 1–1

Creating a Microsoft Account and Signing in to Visio

Before You Begin

Visio Professional 2013 is installed on your computer and has been activated.

 Note: Activities may vary slightly if the software vendor has issued digital updates. Your instructor will notify you of any changes.

Scenario

Before jumping into Visio, you will create a new Microsoft account that you can use during this course without affecting any existing Microsoft accounts you may own. This account is yours to keep and, if you wish, to use after the course.

1. Create a new Microsoft account.
   a) Open Internet Explorer.
   b) Navigate to *https://signup.live.com/signup.aspx*
   c) On the **Create an account** page, in the **Name** fields, type your first and last name.
   d) Below the **User name** field, select the **Or get a new email address** link.
      The appearance of the **User name** field changes.
   e) In the **User name** field after the at sign (@), verify that **outlook.com** is selected as the domain.
   f) In the **User name** field before the at sign (@), type your initials and the eight numerals that represent the current date.
   g) Press the **Tab** key.
      Microsoft displays a message that your desired user name is available.

   ▮▮ Microsoft

   # Create an account

   You can use any email address as the user name for your new Microsoft account, including addresses from Outlook.com, Yahoo! or Gmail. If you already sign in to a Windows PC, tablet, or phone, Xbox Live, Outlook.com, or OneDrive, use that account to sign in.

   Name

Your	Name

   ✓ yn01092014@outlook.com is available.

   User name

yn01092014	@	outlook.com	▾

   Or use your favorite email

   Create a Microsoft account to get a new email inbox and sign in to all Microsoft services.

   h) Write your user name here:

   _____@outlook.com

   i) In the **Create password** and **Reenter password** fields, type your street address with no spaces (for example, *3535WintonPlace*)

j) Write your password here:

_____

k) In the **Country/region** field, verify that the correct country is selected.
l) If a **ZIP code** or **Postal code** field is visible, type the code.
m) In the **Birthdate** fields, select **Month, Day,** and **Year** of your birth.
n) In the **Gender** drop-down field, make a selection.

o) In the **Country code** field, verify that the correct country and code is selected.
p) In the **Phone number** field, type a mobile or other phone number.
q) In the **Alternative email** address field, type another personal or business email address you own.
r) Type the human-readable text you see on the screen.
    Even if some of the letters appear to be uppercase, type them lowercase.

s) If desired, uncheck **Send me promotional offers from Microsoft.**

Help us protect your info

Your phone number helps us keep your account secure.

Country code

United States (+1)

Phone number

555-555-5555

Alternate email address

youname@email.tld

We want to make sure that a real person is creating an account.

Enter the characters you see
New | Audio

3ᴸᵛ5S8S4

The characters didn't match the picture. Please try again.

3cv5s8s4

☑ Send me promotional offers from Microsoft. You can unsubscribe at any time.

Click **Create account** to agree to the Microsoft Services Agreement and privacy and cookies statement.

Create account

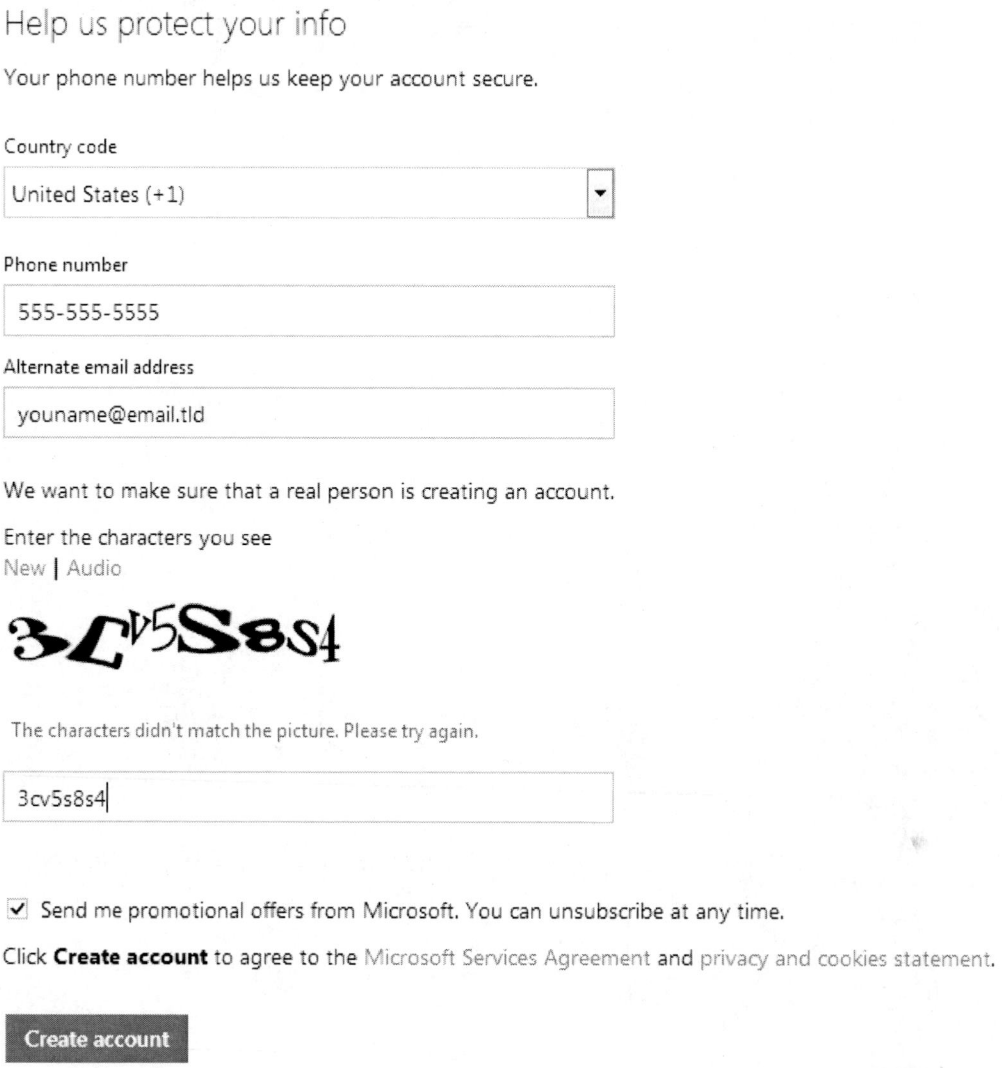

t) Select the **Create account** button.
    Microsoft creates your account and displays the **Microsoft account** page.

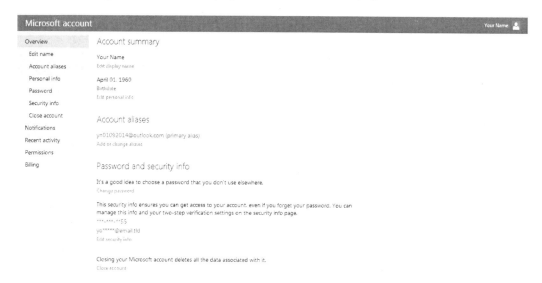

u) Close Internet Explorer.

2. Open Visio.

    a) If you are on the Windows 8.1 **Start** screen, select the **Visio** tile.

    b) If you are on the Windows 8.1 **Desktop**, select the **Visio** icon on the **Desktop** or **Taskbar**.

3. Sign in to Visio with your new Microsoft account.

    a) On the Visio start screen, in the upper-right corner, if Visio isn't signed in to a Microsoft account,
        select **Sign in to get the most out of Office**.

Sign in to get the most out of Office

Learn more

b) If Visio is already signed into a Microsoft account, select **Switch account**.

c) In the **Sign in** dialog box, type the new Outlook email address you created in step 1 and select **Next**.

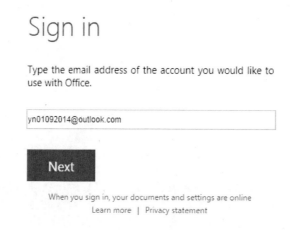

After a brief delay, a **Password** field will appear.

d) Type the password you used in step 1 and select **Sign in**.

Your Microsoft account appears in the upper-right corner of the Visio start screen.

4. Leave the Visio start screen open for the next activity.

TOPIC B

Work with Shape Styles

Whenever you create a new drawing from a Visio template, it will have a certain look and feel applied to it. However, the default graphic style may not be the best one for your needs. All the shapes might be one color, but you want to use several colors. The lines may not be thick enough. Perhaps you want the shapes to have a glow or shadow. The **Shape Style** tools on Visio's **HOME** tab enable you to tweak shapes to suite your sense of aesthetics.

Shape Quick Styles

In *Microsoft® Visio® 2013: Part 1*, you learned how to apply **Themes** and **Variants** to your drawings —both of which are located on the **DESIGN** tab. A *theme* is a combination of fill, line, and effect attributes that harmonize and are applied to the whole drawing. A *variant* is a version of a theme that has different visual attributes. Each theme has four variants. When you select a theme and variant, Visio automatically applies it to all the shapes in your drawing.

There are times, however, when you'll want some of the individual shapes in a drawing to stand out from the rest. For example, you might want marketing shapes to have one style and sales shapes to have another style. **Shape Quick Styles** enable you to do this.

Shape Quick Styles are designed to harmonize with the overall theme and variant of your drawing. Using **Shape Quick Styles** helps ensure that your drawing retains a professional look.

You'll find **Shape Quick Styles** on the **HOME** tab. If the Visio window is narrow, you'll see a **Quick Styles** button; selecting it will display a gallery of **Shape Quick Styles**. However, if the Visio window is wide, you'll see the first row of **Shape Quick Styles** on the ribbon; selecting the **More** icon will display the entire gallery.

Figure 1-3: The Shape Quick Styles gallery.

At the bottom of the **Shape Quick Styles** gallery you'll see two options. If the **Allow Themes** option is checked, the selected shapes will change when you change the theme, variant, or quick style. However, if you check the **Remove Themes** option, the theme, variant, and quick style will be removed from the shapes. You'll no longer be able to apply quick styles to the shapes and any changes to the drawing's theme or variant will not affect the shapes. However, you'll still be able to manually change the shapes' fill, line, and effect attributed.

Fill

The **Fill** command—which is located in **Shape Styles** group on the **HOME** tab—enables you to manually apply different fill attributes to a shape from those assigned by the theme, variant, and quick style. Select the **Fill** button to open the **Fill** gallery. This gallery is similar to the **Fill** gallery you may have used in other Microsoft Office applications.

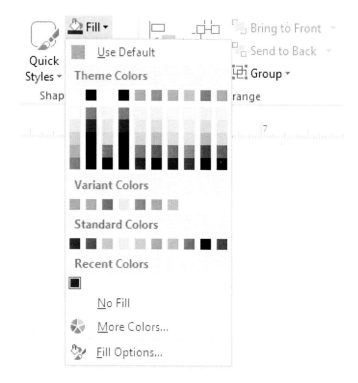

Figure 1-4: The Fill gallery.

This table explains the options available from the **Fill** gallery.

Option	Explanation
Use Default	The default fill attributes of the theme and variant applied to the drawing.
Theme Colors	A palette of fill colors that harmonize with the theme applied to the drawing.
Variant Colors	A palette of fill colors that harmonize with the variant applied to the drawing.
Standard Colors	A palette of basic fill colors.
Recent Colors	A palette of fill colors you recently applied to other shapes.
No Fill	Removes all fill attributes from the selected shapes.
More Colors	Opens a **Color** dialog box so that you can select from a larger palette of standard fill colors or mix a custom fill color.
Fill Options	Opens the **Format Shape** window. In the **FILL** section of the window, you can apply a **Gradient fill** or a **Pattern fill** to the selected shapes.

If you manually apply a fill attribute to a shape, it will stay that way even if you change the drawing's theme and variant.

Line

The **Line** command—which is located in **Shape Styles** group on the **HOME** tab—enables you to manually apply different line attributes to a shape from those assigned by the theme, variant, and quick style. Select the **Line** button to open the **Line** gallery. This gallery is similar to the **Line** gallery you may have used in other Microsoft Office applications.

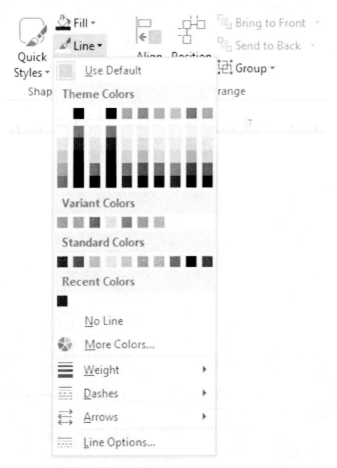

Figure 1-5: The Line gallery.

This table explains the options available from the **Line** gallery.

Option	Explanation
Use Default	The default line attributes of the theme and variant applied to the drawing.
Theme Colors	A palette of line colors that harmonize with the theme applied to the drawing.
Variant Colors	A palette of line colors that harmonize with the variant applied to the drawing.
Standard Colors	A palette of basic line colors.
Recent Colors	A palette of line colors you recently applied to other shapes.
No Line	Removes all line attributes from the selected shapes.
More Colors	Opens a **Color** dialog box so that you can select from a larger palette of standard line colors or mix a custom line color.
Weight	Changes the thickness of the line—ranging from ¼ **pt.** to **6 pt.**
Dashes	Changes the dash style of the line.
Arrows	Changes the arrow head style at the beginning and end of the line.

Option	Explanation
Line Options	Opens the **Format Shape** window. In the **LINE** section of the window, you can apply a number of additional line attributes to the selected shapes.

If you manually apply a line attribute to a shape, it will stay that way even if you change the drawing's theme and variant.

Effects

The **Effects** command—which is located in **Shape Styles** group on the **HOME** tab—enables you to manually apply different effects to a shape from those assigned by the theme, variant, and quick style. Select the **Effects** button to open the **Effects** gallery. This gallery is similar to the **Effects** gallery you may have used in other Microsoft Office applications.

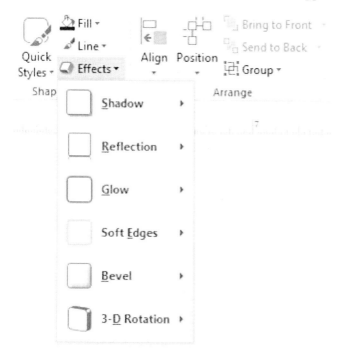

Figure 1-6: The Effects menu.

This table explains the options available from the **Effects** gallery.

Option	Explanation
Shadow	This opens a gallery of shadow options grouped into **Outer**, **Inner**, and **Perspective**. The gallery includes a **Shadow Options** choice that opens the **Format Shape** window to the **SHADOW** section.
Reflection	This opens a gallery of reflection options. The gallery includes a **Reflection Options** choice that opens the **Format Shape** window to the **REFLECTION** section.
Glow	This opens a gallery of glow colors and thicknesses. The gallery includes a **Glow Options** choice that opens the **Format Shape** window to the **GLOW** section.

Option	Explanation
Soft Edges	This changes the thickness of the blur around the edges of shapes—with options ranging from **No Soft Edges** to **50 Point**. The gallery includes **Soft Edges Options** choice that opens the **Format Shape** window to the **SOFT EDGED** section.
Bevel	This opens a gallery of bevel types.
3-D Rotation	This opens a gallery of rotation options grouped into **Parallel**, **Perspective**, and **Oblique** sections.

If you manually apply an effect attribute to a shape, it will stay that way even if you change the drawing's theme and variant.

 Note: Effects should be used sparingly. While a single effect used judiciously can enhance your drawing, multiple effects are likely to make your drawing less polished.

 Access the Checklist tile on your LogicalCHOICE course screen for reference information and job aids on How to Work with Shape Styles.

ACTIVITY 1-2
Working with Shape Styles

Data File

C:\091115Data\Enhancing the Look of Drawings\EE Producing and Consuming Countries.vsdx

Before You Begin

You are on the Visio start screen.

Scenario

You were recently hired as a graphic designer employed by Emerald Epicure—an online vendor of high-quality olive oils. You report to Mary Kaplan, the vice president of marketing. However, because your company is small, you are a shared resource supporting all departments as needed.

 Note: Employees frequently use "EE" as an unofficial abbreviation for Emerald Epicure.

You used Microsoft Visio at your last company and found it very useful. Based on the tasks you anticipate performing at EE, you requested and received permission to purchase Visio Professional 2013.

After installing Visio, you decide to use it for one of your tasks. Mary Kaplan asked you to create a map showing the countries that produce and consume EE's olive oils. Yesterday, you drafted a drawing, and applied a theme and variant. However, it's still rather plain. Today, you want to use Shape Style tools to enhance the map.

1. Open the draft map.
   a) On the Visio start screen, in the **Recent** section, select **Open Other Drawings**.

b) On the **Open** screen, select **Computer**.

c) Select **Browse**.

d) In the **Open** dialog box, navigate to **C:\091115Data\Enhancing the Look of Drawings** and double-click **EE Producing and Consuming Countries.vsdx**.

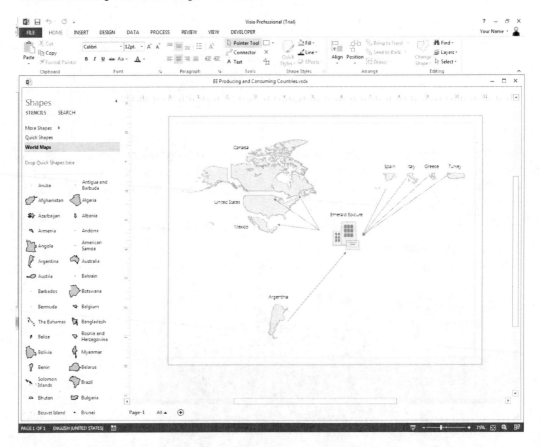

2. Apply a Quick Style to the Emerald Epicure shape.
   a) Select the **Emerald Epicure** shape.
   b) On the ribbon, select **HOME→Shape Styles→Quick Styles**.

c) From the **Quick Styles** menu, in the **Theme Styles** section, select the option that is in the fifth row and fourth column (**Focused Effect - Orange, Variant Accent 4**).

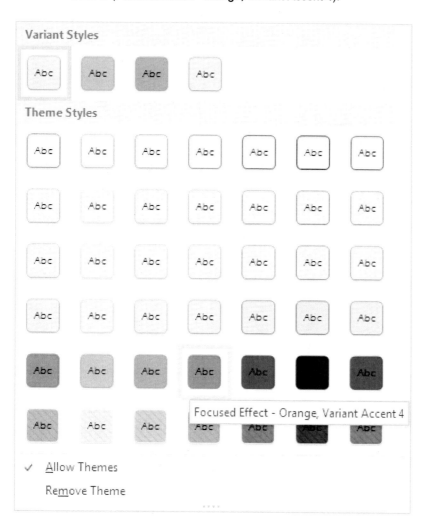

3. Change the fill of the producing countries to green and fill of the exporting countries to red.
   a) Select the **Argentina, Spain, Italy, Greece**, and **Turkey** shapes.
      These are the countries that produce olive oil for EE.
   b) On the ribbon, on the **HOME** tab, in the **Shape Styles** group, select **Fill**.

c) In the **Fill** menu, in the **Theme Colors** section, select the option that is in the first row and fifth column (**Green, Accent 1**).

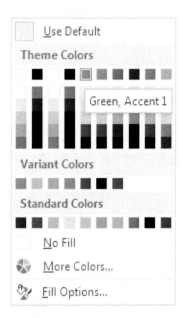

d) Select the **Canada**, **United States,** and **Mexico** shapes.

These are the countries that consume olive oil from EE.

e) In the **Fill** menu, in the **Theme Colors** section, select the option that is in the first row and eighth column (**Red, Accent 4**).

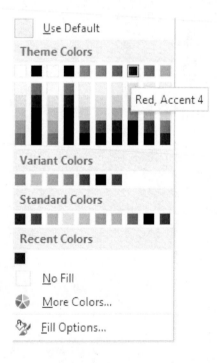

f) Review the map to make sure each shape has the correct color applied to it.

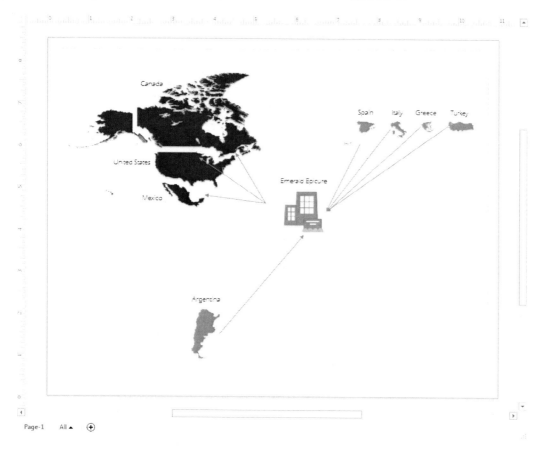

4. Make the lines bolder.

   a) Select all eight lines in the drawing.
   b) On the ribbon, on the **HOME** tab, in the **Shape Styles** group, select **Line**.

c) In the **Line** menu, select **Weight→2¼ pt.**

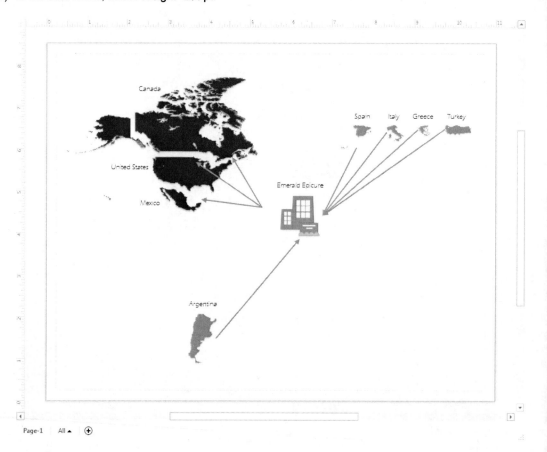

5. Add glow effects to the shapes to make them more visually appealing.

You will give each shape a glow that is the same color as the shape.

a) Select the Emerald Epicure shape.

b) On the ribbon, on the **HOME** tab, in the **Shape Styles** group, select **Effects**.

c) In the **Effects** menu, select **Glow**. Then, in the **Glow Variations** section, select the option that is the fourth row and fifth column (**Orange, 18 pt glow, Accent color 5**).

d) Select the **Argentina, Spain, Italy, Greece,** and **Turkey** shapes.

e) In the **Effects** menu, select **Glow**. Then, in the **Glow Variations** section, select the option that is the fourth row and first column (**Green, 18 pt glow, Accent color 1**).

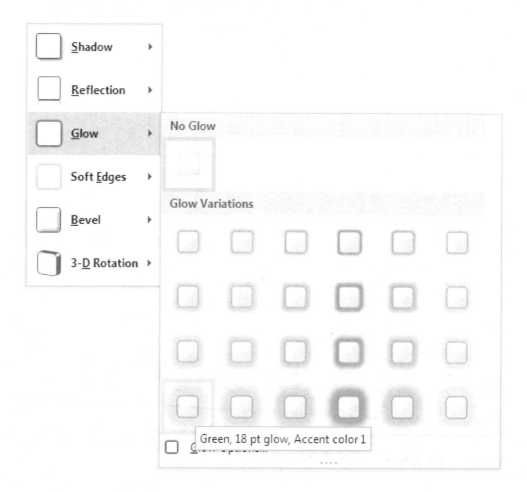

f) Select the **Canada**, **United States**, and **Mexico** shapes.

g) In the **Effects** menu, select **Glow**. Then, in the **Glow Variations** section, select the option that is the fourth row and fourth column (**Red, 18 pt glow, Accent color 4**).

h) Review the map to make sure each shape has the correct glow applied to it.

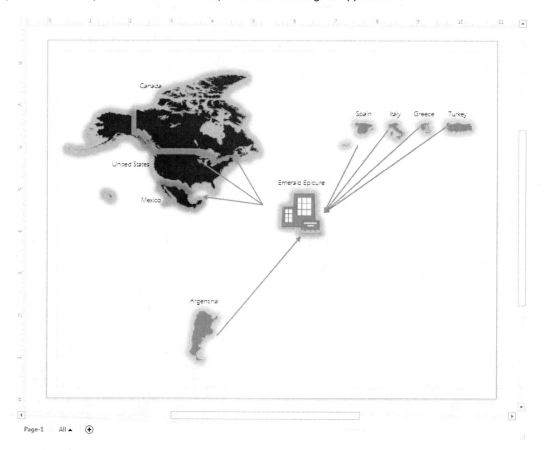

6. Save the enhanced drawing.
   a) On the ribbon, select the **FILE** tab.
   b) On the **Backstage**, select **Save As**.
   c) On the **Save As** screen, verify that **Computer** is selected.

d) Select **Browse**.

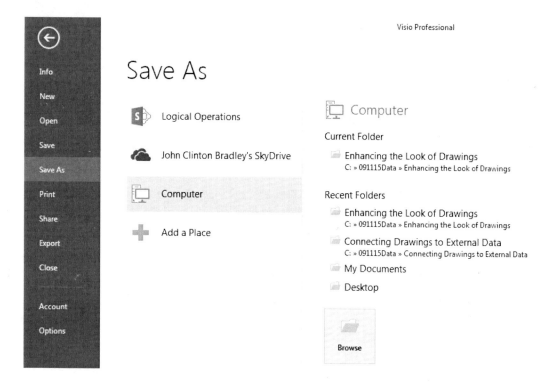

e) In the **Save As** dialog box, verify that the drawing will be saved to the **C:\091115Data\Enhancing the Look of Drawings** folder.

f) In the **File name** field, change the name to *My EE Producing and Consuming Countries.vsdx*

g) Select **Save**.
   Visio closes the **Save As** dialog box.

7. Close the drawing.

TOPIC C

Use 3D Shapes

In most cases, two-dimensional drawings are fine for your needs. However, adding a third dimension can make you drawings more realistic and noticeable. Visio's 3D templates, stencils, shapes, and effects can give a drawing visual volume.

2D vs. 3D Shapes

Most of the shapes in Visio have two dimensions—height and width. In other words, 2D shapes appear flat. However, Visio also includes some shapes with three dimensions—height, width, and depth. 3D shapes appear to be come out from the page.

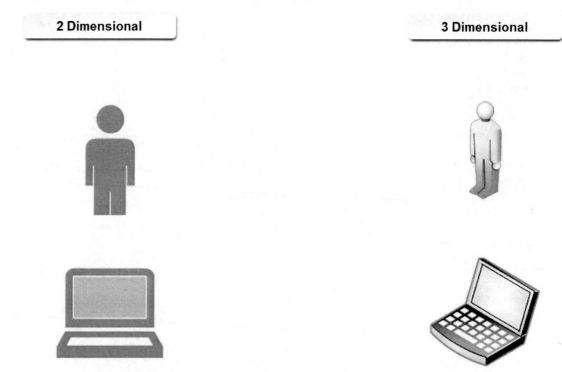

Figure 1-7: Examples of two-dimensional and three-dimensional shapes.

3D shapes are drawn by using *perspective*—which is the art of rendering solid objects on a two-dimensional surface to give the impression of their height, width, and depth when viewed from a particular point.

3D Templates

Visio's online library contains four 3D templates. You can find these templates by searching for "3D" on the Visio **Start** or **New** screen.

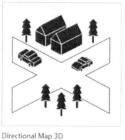

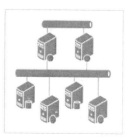

Directional Map 3D   Work Flow Diagram - 3D   Basic Network Diagram - 3D   Detailed Network Diagram - 3D

Figure 1-8: Three-dimensional templates.

3D Stencils

Visio also has a number of 3D stencils. Each 3D template includes one or more 3D stencils. Visio also includes 3D shapes in some 2D stencils—which you can find by searching for "3D" and "perspective" in the **Shapes** window.

Figure 1-9: An example of a stencil with three-dimensional shapes.

This table lists the 3D stencils that are part of each 3D template.

Templates	Stencils
Directional Map 3D	**Directional Map Shapes 3D**

Templates	Stencils
Work Flow Diagram - 3D	Department - 3D
	Work Flow Objects - 3D
Basic Network Diagram - 3D	Computers and Monitors - 3D
	Networks and Peripherals - 3D
Detailed Network Diagram - 3D	Computers and Monitors - 3D
	Detailed Network Diagram - 3D
	Networks and Peripherals - 3D

3-D Format

In the last topic, you were introduced to beveling. You can use this effect to give 2D shapes a 3D appearance. Selecting the **Bevel** option from the **Effects** gallery opens the **Bevel** gallery—which includes a dozen bevel styles. The gallery also includes a **3-D Options** command that opens the **Format Shape** window to the **3-D FORMAT** section.

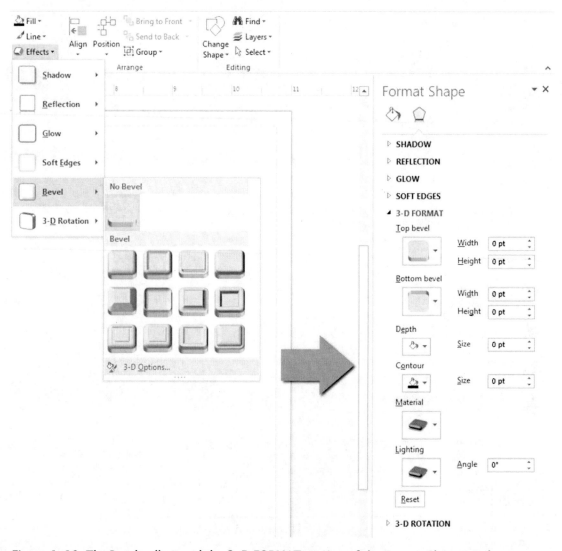

Figure 1-10: The Bevel gallery and the 3-D FORMAT section of the Format Shape window.

This table explains the options on the **3-D FORMAT** section.

Option	Explanation
Top bevel	Shows the same options that are displayed in the **Bevel** gallery. After applying a top bevel to a shape, can change the width and height of the bevel.
Bottom bevel	Shows similar options to those above—but the perspective is shifted from the top to the bottom. After applying a bottom bevel to a shape, can change the width and height of the bevel.
Depth	Enables you to change the color and size of the bevel's depth.
Contour	Enables you to change the color and size of the bevel's contour.
Material	Shows a gallery of different simulated materials—such as **Plastic**, **Metal**, and **Wireframe**.
Lighting	Shows a gallery of different lighting effects—such as **Soft**, **Harsh**, **Sunrise** and **Sunset**. You can also choose an angle for the lighting.
Reset	Removes all 3D formatting.

3-D Rotation

In the last topic, you were introduced to **3-D Rotation**. You can use this effect in conjunction with beveling to give 2D shapes a 3D appearance. Selecting the **3-D Rotation** option from the **Effects** gallery opens the **3-D Rotation** gallery—which includes more than 20 rotation styles. The gallery also includes a **3-D Rotation Options** command that opens the **Format Shape** window to the **3-D ROTATION** section.

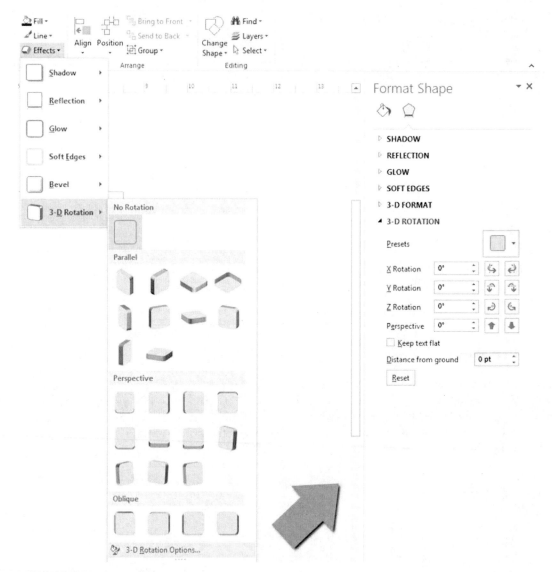

Figure 1–11: The 3–D Rotation gallery and the 3–D ROTATION section of the Format Shape window.

This table explains the options on the **3-D ROTATION** section.

Option	Explanation
Presets	Shows the same options that are displayed in the **3-D Rotation** gallery.
X Rotation	Enables you to rotate a shape along the vertical axis.
Y Rotation	Enables you to rotate a shape along the horizontal axis.
Z Rotation	Enables you to rotate a shape along the depth axis.
Perspective	Enables you to change the apparent viewpoint of the shape.
Keep Text Flat	If the check box is unchecked, the shape's text rotates with the shape. If the check box is checked, the shape's text stays horizontal.
Distance from ground	Enables you to change how high the shape appears above the surface.
Reset	Removes all 3D rotation effects.

Note: Because Visio's 3D shapes are drawn with perspective, you don't need to apply 3D effects to them. In fact, for 3D shapes to look their best, you should avoid changing their **3-D FORMAT** and **3-D ROTATION** options in the **Format Shape** window.

 Note: Visio's 3D shapes don't actually have three dimensions, so they can't be rotated in space. If you try to rotate a 3D shape to show the another side of it, the shape with simply become thinner. However, if you apply 3D effects to a two-dimensional shape, you can rotate the shape in space and see the other side of it.

 Access the Checklist tile on your LogicalCHOICE course screen for reference information and job aids on How to Use 3-D Shapes.

ACTIVITY 1-3
Using 3-D Shapes

Before You Begin

Visio is open.

Scenario

Roxana Addison, the vice president of operations, asked you to create a 3D drawing of the order fulfillment process. Here are the process steps:

1. Place order.
2. Open order.
3. Print packing list/shipping label.
4. Pick products from shelves.
5. Pack products.
6. Ship package.
7. Mark order as shipped.
8. Email shipping notification.

You want to end up with a drawing that looks like this:

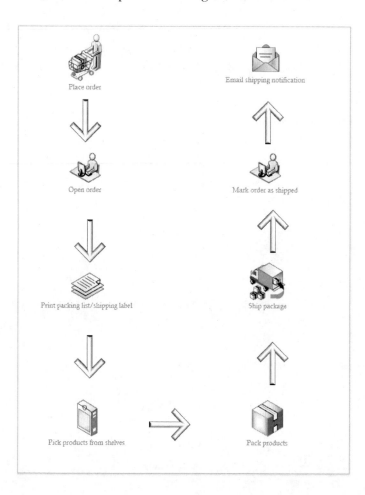

1. Start a new drawing.
   a) On the ribbon, select the **FILE** tab.
   b) On the **Backstage**, select **New**.
   c) On the **New** screen, in the **Search for online templates** field, type *3d* and select the magnifying glass icon.
      Visio finds several 3D templates.
   d) Select **Work Flow Diagram - 3D**.

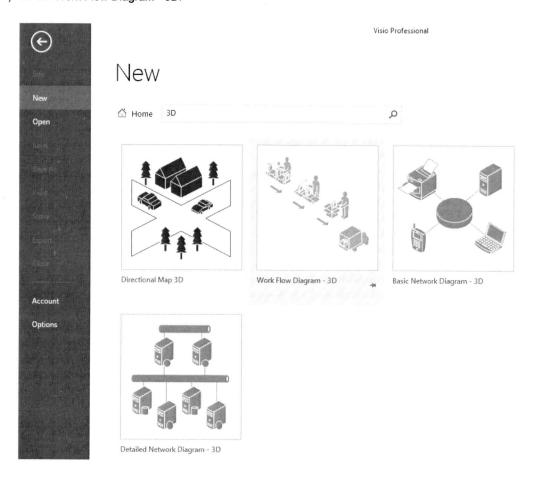

e) In the **Work Flow Diagram - 3D** preview, verify that the **US Units** radio button is selected, and select **Create**.

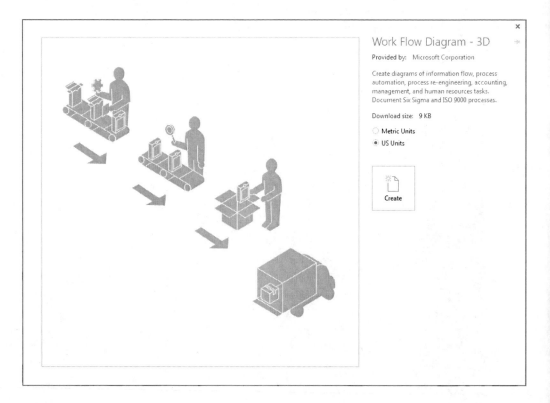

Visio opens a new, blank drawing with four stencils in the **Shapes** window.

2. Add the first step to the drawing.
   a) In the **Shapes** window, select the **Work Flow Objects - 3D** stencil.
   b) Select the **Customer** shape and drag it to the upper left corner of the drawing page.

c) Double-click the new shape on the drawing page, type *Place order*, and press the **Esc** key.

3. In a similar manner, add the remaining steps to the drawing as follows, leaving plenty of space between the shapes:

Step	Stencil	Master Shape	Drag to this Position on Drawing Page	Add this Text Label
2	Work Flow Objects - 3D	User	Below step 1.	*Open order*
3	Work Flow Objects - 3D	Document collection	Below step 2.	*Print packing list/shipping label*
4	Work Flow Objects - 3D	Product	Below step 3.	*Pick products from shelves*

Step	Stencil	Master Shape	Drag to this Position on Drawing Page	Add this Text Label
5	Work Flow Objects - 3D	Box	To the right of step 4.	*Pack products*
6	Departments - 3D	Shipping	Above step 5.	*Ship package*
7	Work Flow Objects - 3D	User	Above step 6.	*Mark order as shipped*
8	Work Flow Objects - 3D	Mail	Above step 7.	*Email shipping notification*

4. Add down arrows to the drawing.
   a) In the **Shapes** window, select the **Arrow Shapes** stencil.
   b) Select the **Modern Arrow** shape and drag it between the first and second steps on the drawing page.
   c) On the ribbon, on the **HOME** tab, in the **Arrange** group, select **Position→Rotate Shapes→Rotate Left 90°**.
   d) Copy the first down arrow and paste to create a second and third down arrow.
   e) Drag the second down arrow between the second and third steps.

f) Drag the third down arrow between the third and fourth steps.

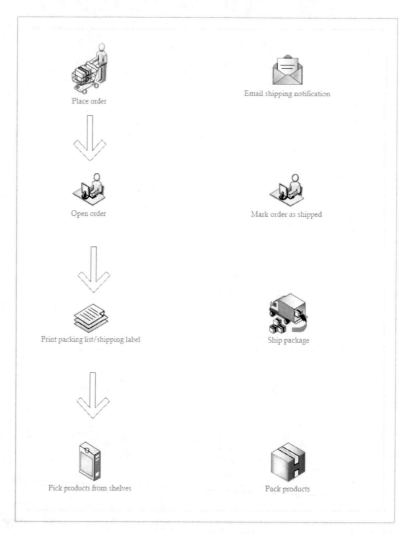

5. Add a right arrow to the drawing.
    a) In the **Shapes** window, in the **Arrow Shapes** stencil, select the **Modern Arrow** shape and drag it between the fourth and fifth steps on the drawing page.

b) On the ribbon, on the **HOME** tab, in the **Arrange** group, select **Position→Rotate Shapes→Flip Horizontal**.

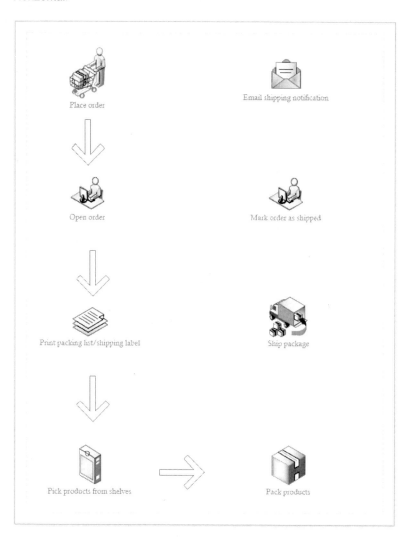

6. Add up arrows to the drawing.

a) In the **Shapes** window, in the **Arrow Shapes** stencil, select the **Modern Arrow** shape and drag it between the fifth and sixth steps on the drawing page.

b) On the ribbon, on the **HOME** tab, in the **Arrange** group, select **Position→Rotate Shapes→Rotate Right 90°**.

c) Copy the first up arrow and paste to create a second and third up arrow.

d) Drag the second up arrow between the sixth and seventh steps.

e) Drag the third up arrow between the seventh and eighth steps.

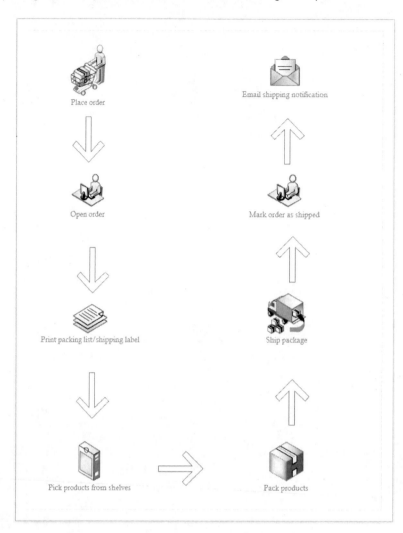

7. Apply a 3D effect to the arrows.
   a) Select all seven arrows.
   b) On the ribbon, on the **HOME** tab, in the **Shape Styles** group, select **Effects**.

c) In the **Effects** menu, select **Bevel→Circle**.

d) Review the drawing to make sure all arrows have the 3D effect.

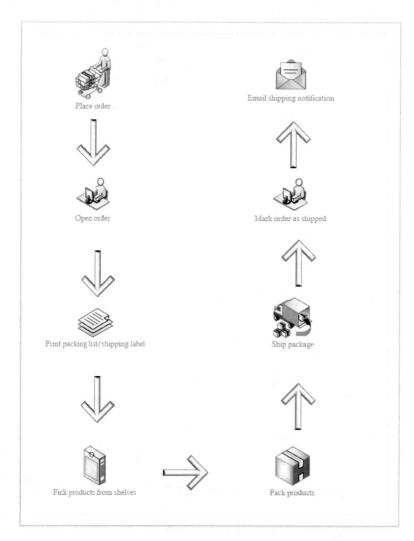

8. Save the drawing.
   a) On the ribbon, select the **FILE** tab.
   b) On the **Backstage**, select **Save As**.
   c) On the **Save As** screen, verify that **Computer** is select.

d) Select the **Browse** button.

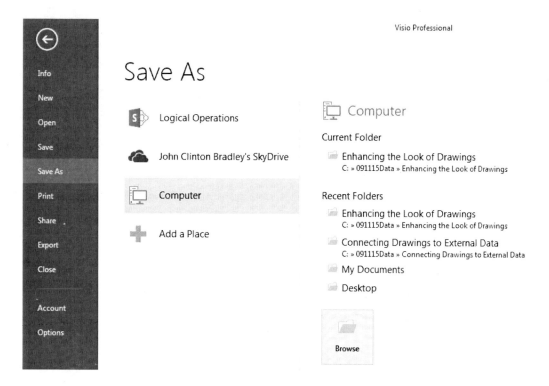

e) In the **Save As** dialog box, navigate to **C:\091115Data\Enhancing the Look of Drawings**.
f) In the **File name** field, change the name to *My EE Order Fulfillment Process.vsdx*
g) Select **Save**.
Visio closes the **Save As** dialog box.

9. Close the drawing.

TOPIC D

Apply Backgrounds, Borders, and Titles

When your create a Visio drawing from a template, the background is plain white. That's fine most of the time; however, the right background can make give your drawing more interesting.

Every great picture needs a great frame. In Visio, great drawings deserve a great border. Borders not only frame a drawing, but they can also convey useful information such as the title of the drawing and when it was made.

Backgrounds

In Visio, you can apply a background to your drawing to make it more attractive. On the **DESIGN** tab, when you select the **Backgrounds** command, Visio displays the **Backgrounds** gallery—which contains ten options. After you apply a background, you can use the **Background Color** gallery to modify the background. The **Background Color** gallery looks and acts just like the **Fill** gallery.

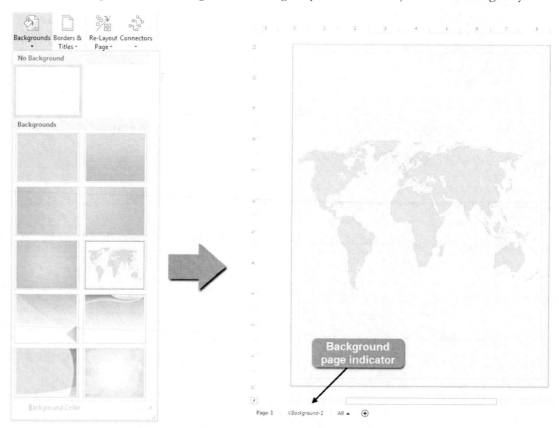

Figure 1–12: The Backgrounds gallery and a background option applied to a drawing.

When you apply a background to a drawing, Visio adds a background page to the page navigator at the bottom of the drawing page. The background page is separate from the drawing page but linked to it. Each drawing page can have its own background.

Borders and Titles

You can also enhance your drawing by applying **Borders & Titles** to it. On the **DESIGN** tab, when you select the **Borders & Titles** command, Visio displays the **Borders and Titles** gallery—which contains ten options.

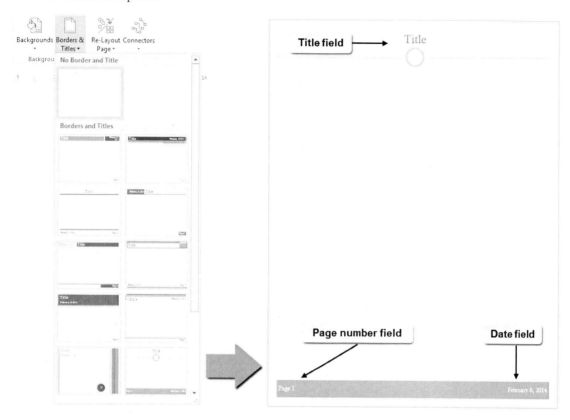

Figure 1-13: The Borders & Titles gallery and a Border and Title option applied to a drawing.

When you apply borders and titles to a drawing, Visio adds them to the background page. The border and title contains three shapes with text:

- **Title.** Double-click the shape to change the placeholder text to your desired title. Delete the field if you don't want a title to appear.
- **Page Number.** This number is automatically populated by Visio based on the page to which it is assigned. Delete the shape if you don't want a page number to appear.
- **Date.** The date is automatically populated by Visio based on the current date. Double-click the shape to replace the current date with a date of your choice. Delete the shape if you don't want a page number to appear.

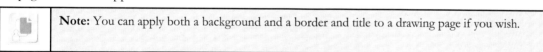
Note: You can apply both a background and a border and title to a drawing page if you wish.

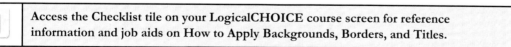
Access the Checklist tile on your LogicalCHOICE course screen for reference information and job aids on How to Apply Backgrounds, Borders, and Titles.

ACTIVITY 1-4
Applying Backgrounds, Borders, and Titles

Data File

C:\091115Data\Enhancing the Look of Drawings\My EE Producing and Consuming Countries.vsdx

Before You Begin

Visio is open.

Scenario

Mary liked the map you created of countries that produce and consume EE's olive oils. However, she has asked you add a background, border, and title to the drawing.

1. Re-open the map.
   a) On the ribbon, select the **FILE** tab.
   b) On the **Backstage**, select **Open**.
   c) On the **Open** screen, in the **Recent Drawings** section, select **My EE Producing and Consuming Countries.vsdx.**

2. Add a background.
   a) On the ribbon, select the **DESIGN** tab.
   b) In the **Backgrounds** group, select the **Backgrounds** command.

c) In the **Backgrounds** menu, select the **Currency** option—which is in the fifth row of the second column.

d) In the **Backgrounds** group, select the **Backgrounds** command.
e) In the **Backgrounds** menu, select the **Background Color** option.

f) In the **Variant Colors** section, select **Tan, Variant Accent 2**—which is the second option from the left.

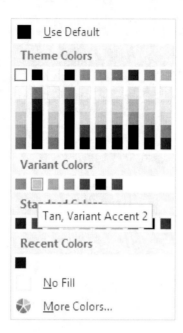

3. Add a border and title.

   a) In the **Backgrounds** group, select the **Borders & Titles** command.

b) In the **Borders and Titles** menu, select the **Blocks** option—which is in the third row of the second column.

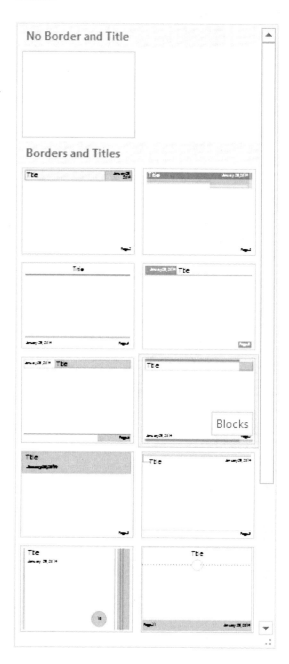

c) If necessary, adjust the position and size of the shapes on the drawing page so that they fit within the selected border and do not overlap the title, date, or page number.

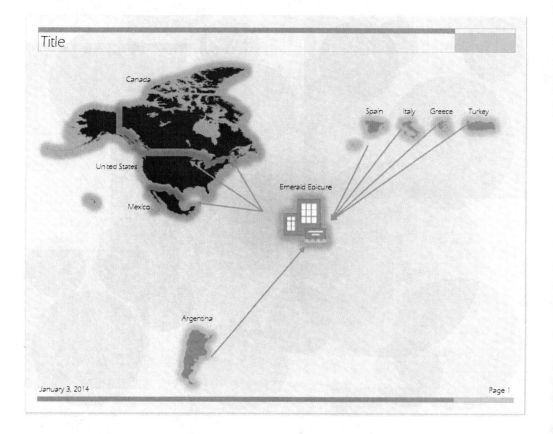

4. Edit the title and footer.

a) Below the drawing page, in the page navigation bar, select **VBackground-1**.
   Visio hides the shapes and connectors and shows the background, border, title, and footers.

b) Double-click the text box containing **Title**, replace the placeholder text by typing *Emerald Epicure Producing and Consuming Countries*, and press the **Esc** key.

Emerald Epicure Producing and Consuming Countries

January 3, 2014   Page 0

c) Double-click the shape containing **Page 0** and press the **Delete** key.

Because this is a single-page drawing, you don't need page numbers.

d) Below the drawing page, select **Page-1**.
   Visio shows the shapes and connectors.

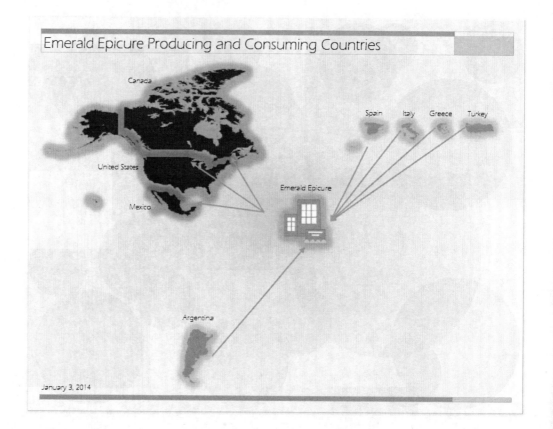

Emerald Epicure Producing and Consuming Countries

| Note: You may need to recenter your drawing by switching to the **VIEW** tab and selecting the **Fit page to current window** icon in the **Status Bar**.

5. Save the drawing by select the **Save** icon in the **Quick Access Toolbar**.

6. Close the drawing.

TOPIC E

Define Shape Styles

Earlier in this lesson you learned how to use Visio's Shape Styles tools to enhance your drawing. Despite the wide range of pre-defined styles, knowing how to define your own style can give you unlimited flexibility to create drawings that look exactly they way you envision them.

Reasons to Define a Style

Earlier in this lesson, you learned about **Shape Quick Styles**. If desired, you can define custom shape styles in Visio. Here are a couple of reasons why you might want to do so:

- None of the quick styles, themes, or variants in Visio met your needs.
- Your company has a style guide. A *style guide* is a set of standards for the writing and design of documents. The implementation of a style guide provides uniformity in style and formatting of documents across the organization.

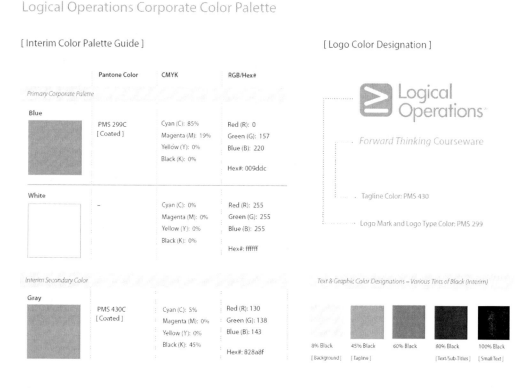

Figure 1–14: An example of a company style guide.

The Define Style and Styles Commands

Before you can define a custom style and use it, you'll need to add two commands to the ribbon— **Define Styles** and **Styles**—by using the **Customize Ribbon** tab in the **Visio Options** dialog box. These commands must be added to a custom group, either on an existing tab or a custom tab.

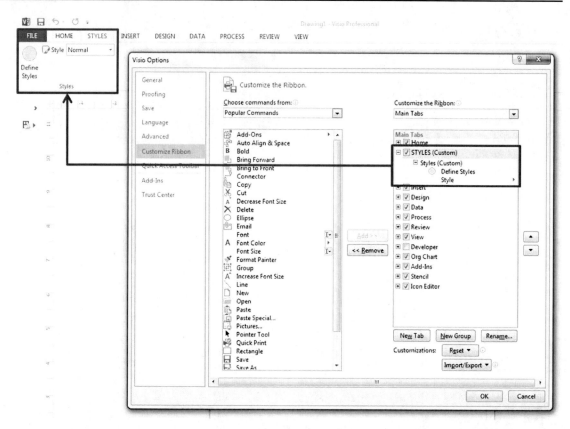

Figure 1–15: Adding the Define Styles and Styles commands to a custom tab and custom group on the ribbon.

 Note: Visio contains three **Style** commands, and this may be confusing. You can't tell the difference between them until you add them to the ribbon. You want the one shown in the figure.

The Define Styles Dialog Box

When you select the **Define Styles** command on the ribbon, Visio opens the **Define Style** dialog box.

Figure 1-16: The Define Styles dialog box.

Once you define a style, you can apply it to a shape by using the **Style** command.

This table describes each element in the **Define Style** dialog box.

Element	Description
Name	When you begin creating a new style, you'll see a **<New style>** placeholder in the field. Type a new style name over this placeholder. If you select the drop-down arrow, you'll see a list of existing styles embedded in the drawing.
Based on	When you begin creating a new style, you'll see **No Style** in this field. If you wish, you can base your new style on an existing style chosen from the drop-down list.
Add	After you name and define the style, select this button to embed the style in your drawing.
Delete	Select this button to delete the style shown in the **Name** field from the drawing.
Rename	Select this button to give the style shown in the **Name** field a new name.
Includes	Use these check boxes to indicate whether or not the new style will apply to **Text**, **Line**, and **Fill** components. If a check box is checked, the style will be applied to that component of a shape. If a check box is unchecked, the style will not be applied to that component of a shape.
Change | Text	When you select this button, Visio displays a **Text** dialog box—in which you can specify **Font**, **Character**, **Paragraph**, **Text Block**, **Tabs**, and **Bullets** attributes.

Element	Description
Change | Shape	When you select this button, Visio displays a **Format Shape** dialog box—in which you can specify **FILL** and **LINE** attributes. This dialog box looks and acts like the **FILL** and **LINE** sections of the **Format Shape** window you learned about earlier.
Hidden Style	If this check box is checked, the custom style won't appear as an option in the **Styles** drop-down list. If this check box is unchecked, the custom style will appear as an option in the **Styles** drop-down list.
Preserve local format on apply	If this check box is checked, the custom style won't overwrite any formatting already applied to the selected shapes. If this check box is unchecked, the custom style will overwrite any formatting already applied to the selected shapes.

Reuse of Custom Styles

When you define custom styles, they do not become part of the Visio program itself. Rather, they become part of the drawing file in which you defined the styles. There are two ways to reuse custom styles in other drawings:

- You can save a drawing that contains custom styles as a Visio Template (*.vstx) file. If you start a new drawing from the template, it will include the custom styles.
- If you copy a shape with a custom style from one drawing and paste the shape into another drawing, the custom style will be also be pasted into the new drawing.

 Note: Make sure that the custom style you are copying from the first drawing doesn't have the same name as an existing style in the second drawing. If both drawings have a style with the same name, the custom style won't paste in to the second drawing. You must rename of the style in either the first or second drawing, and then perform the copy and paste.

 Note: To learn more about enhancing the look of your drawings, you can access the LearnTO **Work With Layers** presentation from the **LearnTO** tile on the LogicalCHOICE Course screen.

 Access the Checklist tile on your LogicalCHOICE course screen for reference information and job aids on How to Define Shape Styles.

ACTIVITY 1-5
Defining Shape Styles

Data File

C:\091115Data\Enhancing the Look of Drawings\EE Flowchart Example.vsdx

Before You Begin

Visio is open.

Scenario

As the new graphic artist at Emerald Epicure, you've noticed that many styles are being used in print and electronic documents. In consultation with Mary Kaplan, vice president for marketing, you developed a simple style guide. Here are the specifications.

Color palette	• Dark Green (Hex #006400 or RGB 0, 100, 0) • Yellow (Hex # FFFF00 or RGB 255, 255, 0) • Black (Hex #000000 or RGB 0, 0, 0) • White (Hex #FFFFFF or RGB 255, 255, 255)
Text	• Titles: Arial Bold (14-28 point) • Body: Times New Roman (10-12 point) • Graphics: Arial Italic (10-12 point)

Now you want to define a shape style in Visio that meets these specifications and apply it to a flowchart you created previously.

1. Open the flowchart.
   a) On the ribbon, select the **FILE** tab.
   b) On the **Backstage**, select **Open**.
   c) On the **Open** screen, select the **Computer** option.
   d) Select **Browse**.
   e) In the **Open** dialog box, navigate to **C:\091115Data\Enhancing the Look of Drawings** and double-click **EE Flowchart Example.vsdx**.

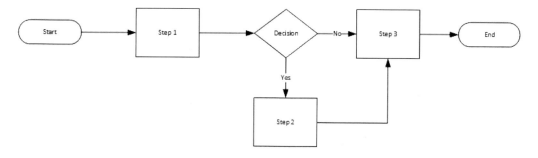

2. Add style commands to the ribbon.
   To do this, you will need to add a new tab, a new group, and two new commands.
   a) On the ribbon, select the **FILE** tab.

b) On the **Backstage**, select **Options**.
c) In the **Visio Options** dialog box, select **Customize Ribbon**.
d) On the right side of the screen, explore the hierarchy of the **Main Tabs** by selecting the plus icons.

Tabs are the first level. Groups are the second level. Commands are the third level. Check marks indicate that a tab is visible on the ribbon.

e) Below the **Customize the Ribbon** list, select the **New Tab** button.
Visio inserts a new tab and new group in the **Customize the Ribbon** list.

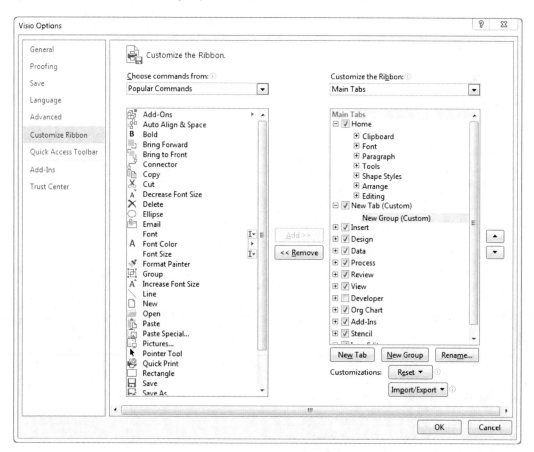

f) With **New Group (Custom)** selected, select the **Rename** button.

g) In the **Rename** dialog box, verify that the **Display name** field is selected, rename **New Group** to *My New Group*, and select **OK**.

h) Select **New Tab (Custom)** and select **Rename**.

i) In the **Rename** dialog box, verify that the **Display name** field is selected, rename **New Tab** to *My New Tab*, and select **OK**.

j) Select the **My New Group (Custom)** group again.

k) At the top of the **Choose commands from** list, select the **Popular Commands** drop-down field and select **All Commands**.

l) Scroll down the list of commands, select the **Define Styles** command, and select **Add**.

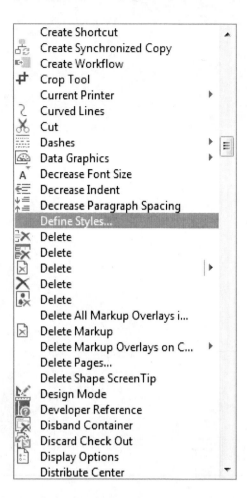

Visio adds the **Define Styles** command to **My New Group** on the right side.

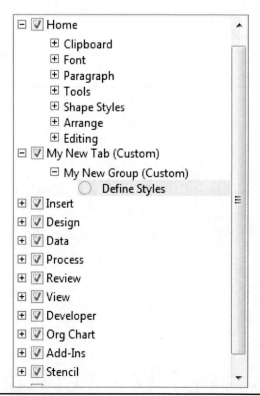

m) On the left side, scroll down the list of commands and select the second **Style** command.

Take care to select the second **Style** command. The first and third **Style** commands aren't needed for this activity.

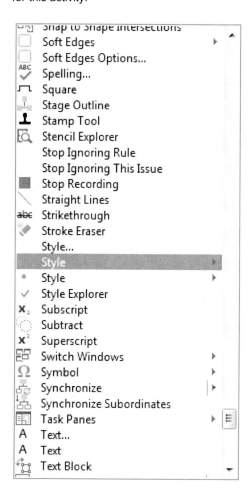

n) Select the **Add** button.
Visio adds the **Style** command to **My New Group** on the right side.

o) Select **OK**.
p) On the ribbon, select **My New Tab** tab to see the new group and new commands.

3. Define a shape style.
    a) On the ribbon, on **My New Tab**, select the **Define Styles** command.
    b) In the **Define Styles** dialog box, verify that the **Name** field is selected, and replace **<New Style>** with *EE Shape Style*

c) In the **Based on** field, verify that **No Style** is selected.

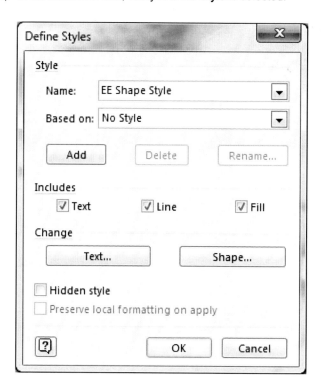

d) Select the **Text** button.

Take care not to select the **Text** check box in the **Includes** section.

e) In the **Text** dialog box, select the **Font** field and select the **Arial** option.

f) Select the **Style** field and select the **Italic** option.

g) Select the **Size** field and select the **10 pt.** option.

h) Select the **Color** field and, in the **Standard Colors** section, select **Yellow**.

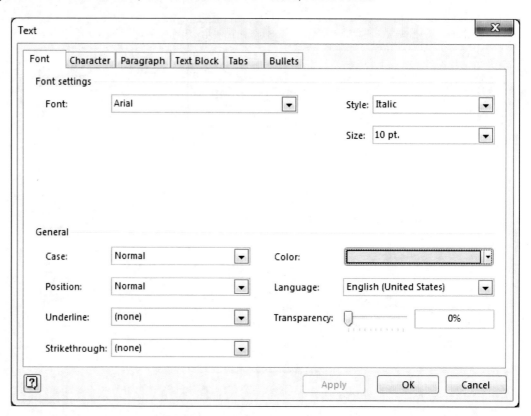

i) Select **OK** to close the **Text** dialog box.
j) In the **Define Styles** dialog box, select the **Shape** button.

k) In the **Format Shape** window, select **FILL**.

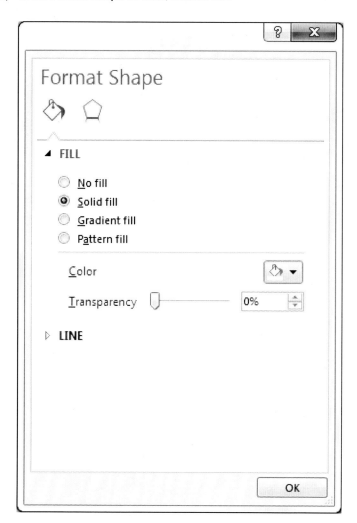

l) Verify that the **Solid fill** radio button is selected.

m) Select the **Fill Color** icon 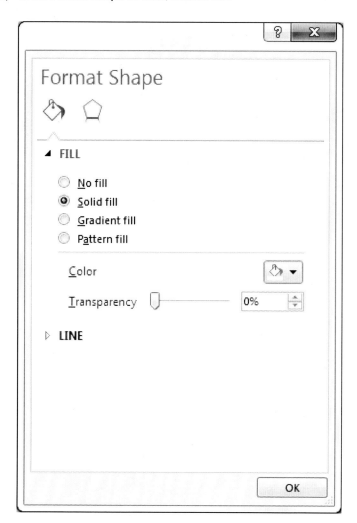 and the **More Colors** option.

n) In the **Colors** dialog box, select the **Custom** tab.

o) Select the **Red** field and change the value to **0**.

p) Select the **Green** field and change the value to **100**.

q) Select the **Blue** field and change the value to **0**.

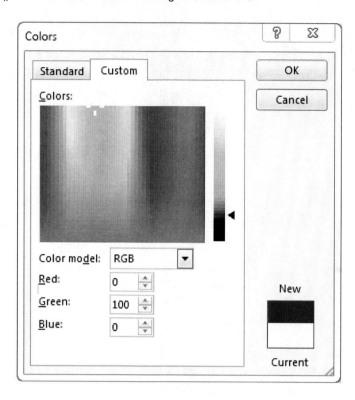

r) Select **OK** to close the **Colors** dialog box.

s) In the **Format Shape** dialog box, select **LINE**.

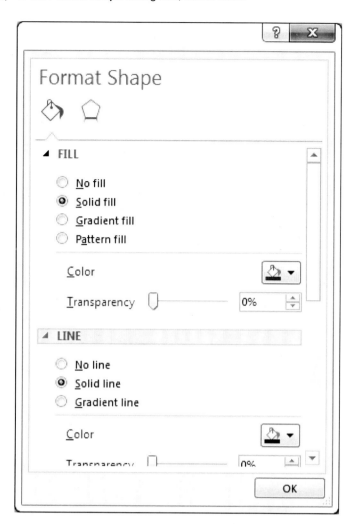

t) Select the **Outline color** icon .
u) In the **Recent Colors** section, select the dark green swatch.
v) Select **OK** to close the **Format Shape** dialog box.
w) Select **Add** to add the style to the drawing.

At this point, you could define another style if you wished.

x) Select **OK** to close the **Define Styles** dialog box.

4. Apply the new style to a shape.

a) On the drawing page, select all of the shapes, but none of the connectors.

b) On the ribbon, on **My New Tab**, select the **Style** command and select the **EE Shape Style** option.

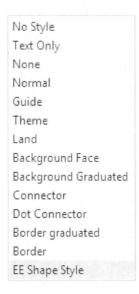

c) Review the drawing to ensure that the style was applied to all of the shapes.

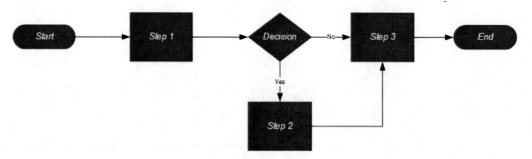

5. Save the drawing in the **C:\091115Data\Enhancing the Look of Drawings** folder as *My EE Flowchart Example.vsdx*

6. Close the drawing.

Summary

In this lesson, you learned how to use Visio to give your drawings greater visual appeal. You tweaked shapes to suit your sense of aesthetics. You applied 3D templates, stencils, shapes, and effects to give your drawings visual volume. You added backgrounds, borders, and titles to make drawings more interesting and informative. Finally, you defined your own styles to create drawings that look exactly they way you envision them.

How might you enhance drawings you have already created?

What is your company's style? How can you apply your company's style to Visio drawings?

 Note: Check your LogicalCHOICE Course screen for opportunities to interact with your classmates, peers, and the larger LogicalCHOICE online community about the topics covered in this course or other topics you are interested in. From the Course screen you can also access available resources for a more continuous learning experience.

2 | Creating Shapes, Stencils, and Templates

Lesson time: 30 minutes

Lesson Objectives

In this lesson, you will create custom shapes, stencils, and templates. You will:

- Create a simple custom shape.
- Create a custom stencil.
- Create a custom template.

Lesson Introduction

Visio's online library gives you access to a vast number of templates, stencils, and shapes. For most jobs, these resources are fine. Sometimes, however, you'll need to create custom shapes, stencils, and templates.

TOPIC A

Create Simple Custom Shapes

Shapes are the basic building blocks of Visio. Adding custom shapes to Visio enables you to produce drawings that reflect the uniqueness of your company.

Shapes, Stencils, and Templates

You're already experienced at using Visio's built-in shapes, stencils, and templates. To begin this lesson, you need to understand how these objects relate to one another:

*   A **shape** is the basic building block of Visio. There are two kinds of shapes—master shapes and regular shapes—which will be discussed later.
*   A Visio **stencil** consists of one or more master shapes.
*   A Visio **template** consists of one or more stencils.

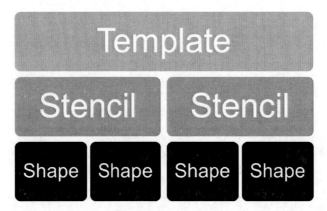

Figure 2–1: The relationship among Visio shapes, stencils, and templates.

Visio File Formats

Visio 2013 saves files in three formats:

*   **Visio Drawing (*.vsdx).** This the format you will use the most often. It's the default when you save a drawing.
*   **Visio Stencil (*.vssx).** This is the format you will use to save shapes in a reusable stencil.
*   **Visio Template (*.vstx).** This is the format you use to save a drawing as a reusable template.

Visio 2003 through 2010 also saved files in three formats:

*   **Visio Drawing (*.vsd)**
*   **Visio Stencil (*.vss)**
*   **Visio Template (*.vst)**

The difference between the new and old Visio file formats is more than just the addition of the letter x at the end of the file extensions. Visio 2013 uses an entirely different file structure based on Extensible Markup Language (XML). Visio 2003–2010 used a binary file structure. The new XML file structure allows developers to more easily create third-party applications that work with Visio files.

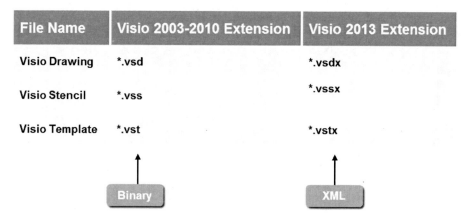

File Name	Visio 2003-2010 Extension	Visio 2013 Extension
Visio Drawing	*.vsd	*.vsdx
Visio Stencil	*.vss	*.vssx
Visio Template	*.vst	*.vstx

Figure 2-2: Comparing old and new Visio file formats.

If you encounter old binary Visio files, you can open them in Visio 2013 and save them in the new XML format. You can also save Visio 2013 files in the old binary format if you are working with someone who has a legacy version of Visio.

Simple Custom Shapes

Although Visio comes packed with shapes, you can add your own shapes to the program. Just about any graphic can be imported into Visio and used as a shape.

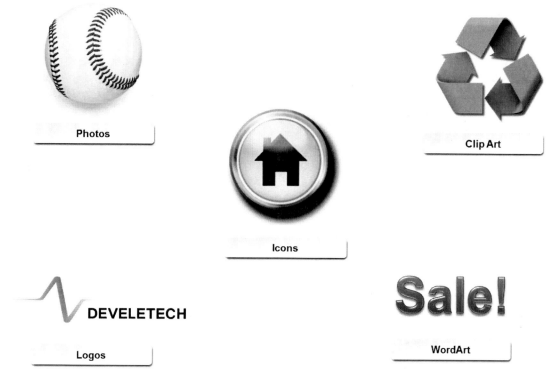

Figure 2-3: Examples of custom shapes.

Vector vs. Raster Graphics

Visio shapes can either be vector or raster graphics.

Vector graphics are composed of mathematically defined geometric shapes, so you can make them larger (or smaller) in Visio without changing their visual quality. Here are some common vector graphic formats:

- Adobe® Illustrator® (*.ai)
- Scalable Vector Graphic (*svg)
- Windows® Metafile (*wmf)

Raster graphics are composed of tiny squares (pixels). If you make them larger (or smaller) than their original size in Visio, they may lose visual quality. Here are some common raster graphic formats:

- Graphics Interchange Format (*.gif)
- Joint Photographic Experts Group (*.jpg or *.jpeg)
- Portable Network Graphic (*.png)
- Tagged Image File Format (*.tif or *.tiff)
- Windows Bitmap (*.bpm)

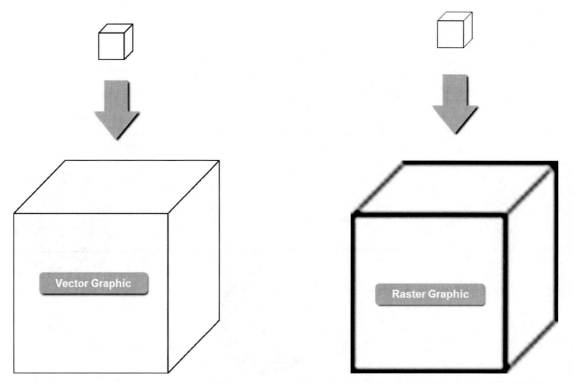

Figure 2-4: What happens when vector and raster graphics are enlarged.

Given the limitations of raster graphics, it's best to use custom vector graphics in Visio whenever possible.

 Note: You can use the drawing tools in Microsoft® Word, PowerPoint®, or Excel® to create vector graphics. You can also use the **Shape Design** tools in Visio. You'll learn how to do this later in the course.

When to Create a Custom Shape

Here are a couple of situations when you might need to create a simple custom shape:

- None of the Visio master shapes meet your needs.
- You have a logo or other graphic—such as product images—you intend to use repeatedly.

Ways to Create a Simple Custom Shape

You can create simple custom shapes in Visio by using these methods:

*   Insert pictures (graphics from your computer or network) or online pictures (graphics from Office.com, Bing, or your OneDrive) into your Visio drawing.
*   Copy images from another program (such as Word or PowerPoint) and paste them into your Visio drawing.

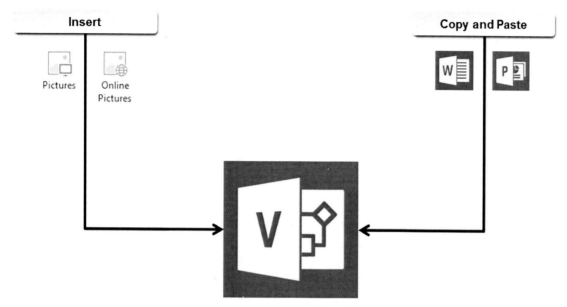

Figure 2-5: Two methods for creating simple custom shapes in Visio.

The Favorites Stencil

You can easily save simple custom shapes by adding them to the **Favorites** stencil, which you can access from the **Shapes** window by selecting **More Shapes→My Shapes→Favorites**. After you save a custom shape in the **Favorites** stencil, you'll be able to access from any drawing.

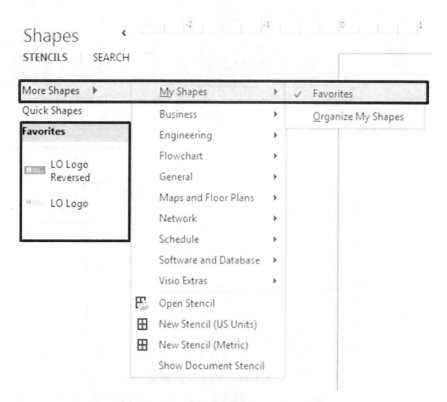

Figure 2-6: Accessing the Favorites stencil.

Master and Regular Shapes

As mentioned earlier in this topic, Visio has two kinds of shapes—master shapes and regular shapes. Master shapes reside in stencils and regular shapes reside on drawing pages. When you drag a regular shape to a stencil, it becomes a master shape. When you drag a master shape to the drawing page, a copy of it becomes a regular shape.

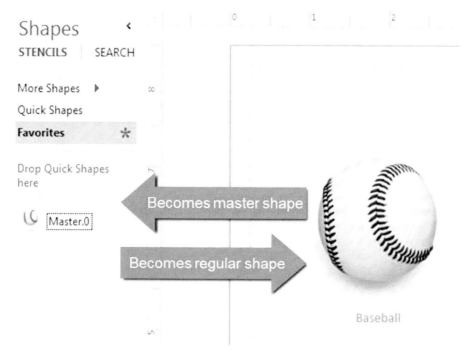

Figure 2-7: The relationship between master shapes and regular shapes.

Stencil States

The **Favorites** stencil and custom stencils have three states, which are explained in this table.

Stencil State	Explanation
Locked Favorites	Shapes can't be added to the stencil. If you attempt to add a shape to the stencil, Visio will ask if you want to edit the stencil. You can also unlock a stencil by right-clicking the name of the stencil and selecting **Edit Stencil**.
Edit Favorites *	A red asterisk indicates that the stencil is in edit mode. You can add new master shapes to the stencil.
Save Favorites 🖫	A diskette icon indicates that you've made edits to the stencil and you need to save it.

Keep in mind that you add master shapes only to the **Favorites** stencil or a custom stencil. If you attempt to add a master shape to non-custom stencil, Visio will display a message to this effect.

Master Shape Commands

When a stencil is in **Edit** mode, you can perform a number of commands on the master shapes it contains. You can access these commands by right-clicking a master shape.

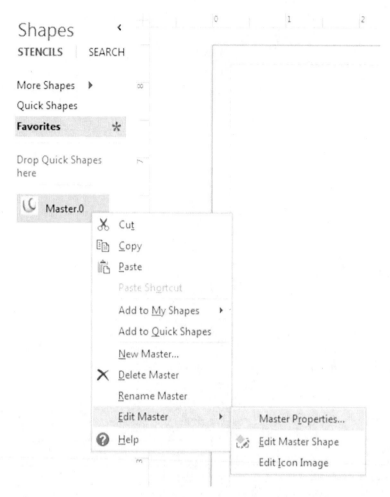

Figure 2–8: Commands related to master shapes.

This table explains each command.

Command	Explanation
Cut	Deletes a shape from the stencil and puts it on the Windows Clipboard.
Copy	Copies a shape from the stencil to the Windows Clipboard.
Paste	Pastes a shape from the Windows Clipboard into the stencil.
Add to My Shapes	Enables you to copy a shape to another stencil.
Add to Quick Shapes	Enables you to move a shape to the **Quick Shapes** section of the current stencil.
New Master	Creates a new master shape in the stencil.
Delete Master	Deletes a shape form the stencil.
Rename Master	Enables you rename a master shape in the stencil.
Edit Master	Displays the **Master Properties**, **Edit Master Shape**, and **Edit Icon Image** commands.
Master Properties	Opens a **Master Properties** dialog box where you can change the shape's **Name**, **Prompt**, **Icon size**, and other attributes.

Command	Explanation
Edit Master Shape	Opens the shape in a drawing page so that you can modify it.
Edit Icon Image	Opens the **Icon Editor** so that you can modify the shape's icon.

 Access the Checklist tile on your LogicalCHOICE course screen for reference information and job aids on How to Create Simple Custom Shapes.

ACTIVITY 2–1
Creating Simple Custom Shapes

Data File
C:\091115Data\Creating Shapes, Stencils, and Templates\EE Logo.png

Before You Begin
Visio is open.

Scenario
You'll be using the Emerald Epicure logo on most of the drawings you create with Visio. Rather than importing the logo each time you need it, you decide to create a custom shape master for the EE logo.

---

1. Start a new drawing.
   a) On the ribbon, select **FILE**.
   b) On the **Backstage**, select **New**.
   c) On the **New** screen, select the **Blank Drawing** template.

d) In the **Blank Drawing** preview, verify that the **US Units** radio button is selected and select **Create**.

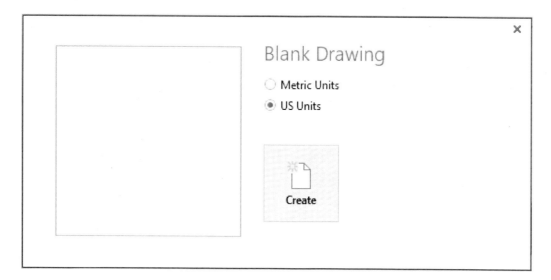

Visio opens a blank drawing.

2. Insert the EE logo into the drawing.
   a) On the ribbon, select the **INSERT** tab.
   b) In the **Illustrations** group, select the **Pictures** command.
   c) In the **Insert Picture** dialog box, navigate to **C:\091115Data\Creating Shapes, Stencils, and Templates** and double-click **EE Logo.png**.

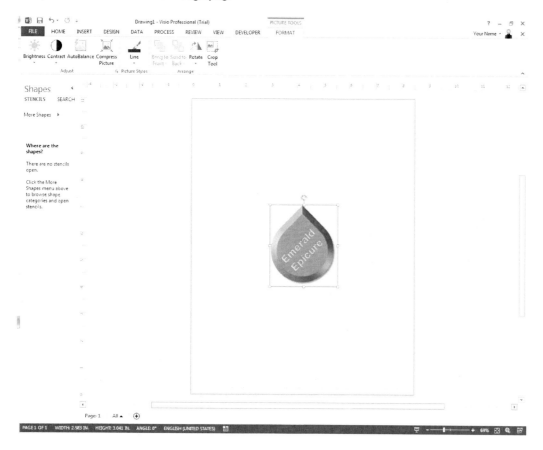

3. Add the EE logo to the **Favorites** stencil.

   a) In the **Shapes** window, select **More Shapes→My Shapes→Favorites**.

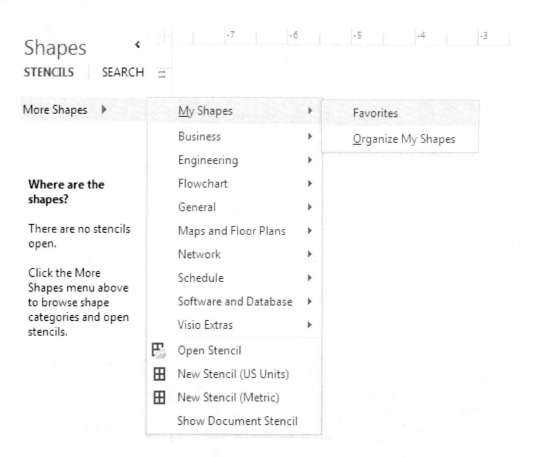

   b) Drag the EE logo from the drawing page to the **Shapes** window and drop it in the blank area below **Drop Quick Shapes here.**
   Visio displays a message asking if you want to edit the stencil.

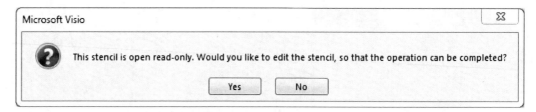

c) In the **Microsoft Visio** dialog box, select **Yes**.

Visio converts the logo to a master shape.

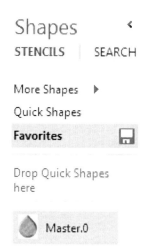

4. Rename the master shape.
    a) Right-click **Master.0**.
    b) In the shortcut menu, select **Rename Master**.
    c) Replace **Master.0** by typing *My EE Logo*

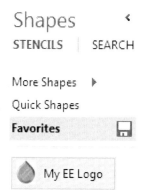

5. Save the master shape in the **Favorites** stencil.
    a) At the top of the **Favorites** stencil, select the **Save Stencil** icon.

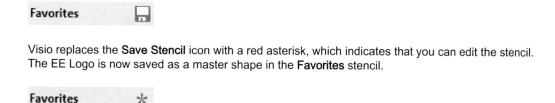

Visio replaces the **Save Stencil** icon with a red asterisk, which indicates that you can edit the stencil. The EE Logo is now saved as a master shape in the **Favorites** stencil.

6. Use the stencil.

a) Drag the **My EE Logo** master shape from the **Shapes** window to the drawing page. Notice that a copy of the Emerald Epicure logo is on the drawing page as a regular shape.

b) In the **Quick Access Toolbar**, select the **Undo** icon ↶ to remove the logo from the drawing page.

7. Leave this drawing open for the next activity.

TOPIC B

Create Custom Stencils

If you add a lot of custom shapes to Visio, you're going to want a way to keep those shapes organized. Custom stencils enable you to put your custom shapes in containers so that you can find and use them when you need them.

New Stencil Commands

Although you can save custom shapes in the **Favorites** stencil, there may be time when you want to save them in a new, custom stencil. For example, you might want to create a stencil for your company that you can share with other employees who use Visio. You can create a new stencil from the **Shapes** window by selecting **More Shapes→New Stencil (US Units)** or **New Stencil (Metric)**.

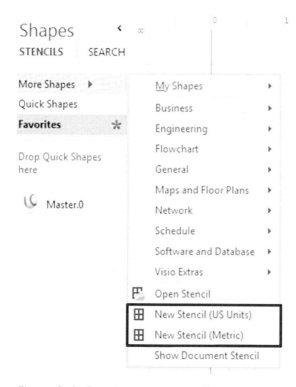

Figure 2-9: Creating a new stencil.

When you select one of the **New Stencil** options, Visio opens a new stencil in the **Shapes** window. Visio automatically gives the stencil a name (such as Stencil7) based on the number of times you've created a new stencil with this installation of Visio. However, you can rename the stencil if you wish. Visio opens the new stencil in **Edit** mode so that you can add shapes to it.

The My Shapes Folder

When Visio is installed on your computer, it creates a **My Shapes** folder in the **My Documents** or **Documents** directory of your computer (depending on whether you are running Windows 7 or Windows 8. During installation, Visio also creates the **Favorites** stencil in the **My Shapes** folder.

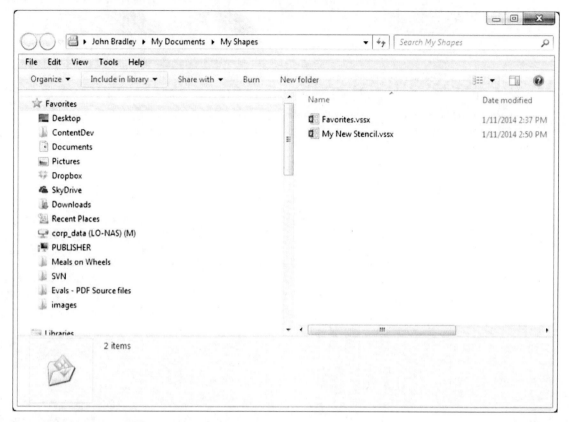

Figure 2-10: The My Shapes folder in Windows 7.

The Stencil Save and Save As Commands

If you right-click a stencil name in the **My Shapes** window, you'll have two options for saving custom stencils:

*   The **Save** option saves the stencil with its current name.
*   The **Save As** option saves the stencil with a new name.

Figure 2-11: Saving a stencil.

By default, Visio saves new stencils in the **My Shapes** folder so that you can easily access them no matter which drawing is open. However, if you wish, you can save stencils in a different location.

The Edit Stencil Command

If a stencil is in **Lock** mode, you can change it to **Edit** mode by right-clicking the stencil name in the **Shapes** windows and selecting the **Edit Stencil** command. If a stencil is in **Edit** mode, you can change it to **Lock** mode by again selecting the **Edit Stencil** command.

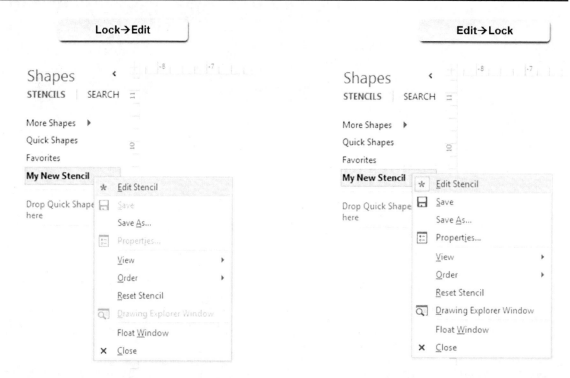

Figure 2-12: Changing a stencil from Lock to Edit mode and from Edit to Lock mode.

 Note: You can't edit the stencils that come with Visio.

The Stencil Properties Dialog Box

While a stencil is in **Edit** mode, you can change its properties by right-clicking the stencil name in the **Shapes** windows and selecting the **Properties** command. The command opens the **Stencil Properties** dialog box to the **Summary** tab.

Figure 2-13: The Stencil Properties dialog box.

The following table explains the primary fields on the **Summary** tab. If you plan to share the stencil with others, it's a good idea to include as much information as possible.

Field	Explanation
Title	If this field is empty, Visio's automatic name is applied to the stencil. If you enter a name in this field, it will change the name of the stencil.
Subject	State the intended purpose of the stencil.
Author	Visio will automatically put your Microsoft account name in this field. However, you can type a different name if you wish.
Manager	Type the name of your supervisor.
Company	Type the organization for which you work.
Language	Visio will automatically insert your Microsoft account language in this field. However, you can select a different language if necessary.

> **Access the Checklist tile on your LogicalCHOICE course screen for reference information and job aids on How to Create a Custom Stencil.**

ACTIVITY 2-2
Creating Custom Stencils

Before You Begin
The drawing from the last activity is open.

Scenario
Now that you have created a master shape for the Emerald Epicure logo, you want to create custom stencil for the EE logo and other master shapes you create for the company.

---

1. Create a new stencil.
   a) In the **Shapes** window, select the **More Shapes** command.
   b) Select the **New Stencil (US Units)** option.

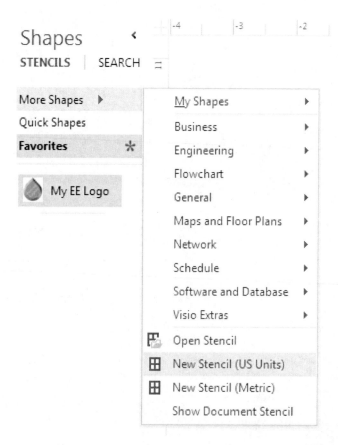

c) In the **Shapes** window, notice that a new stencil appears with a red asterisk, indicating that you can edit the stencil.

 Note: Visio automatically numbers new stencils based on the number of times the command has been activated. If an installation of Visio was previously used to create a stencil, the stencil name will end with a different numeral than 1.

2. Rename the stencil and add other information to the stencil.

Because you can share stencils with other users, you may wish to add additional information to the stencil properties, including a copyright notice if appropriate.

a) In the **Shapes** window, right-click the new stencil name.

b) In the shortcut menu, select **Properties**.

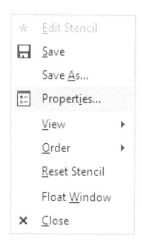

c) In the **Stencil Properties** dialog box, verify that the **Summary** tab is selected.

d) In the **Title** field, type *My EE Stencil*

e) In the **Author** field, notice that your name is already inserted.

f) In the **Manager** field, type *Mary Kaplan*

g) In the **Company** field, type *Emerald Epicure*

h) In the **Comments** field, type *Copyright YYYY Emerald Epicure*, replacing *YYYY* with the current year.

i) Select **OK**.
Notice the custom stencil has a new name in the **Shapes** window and that the red asterisk has been replaced by a diskette icon.

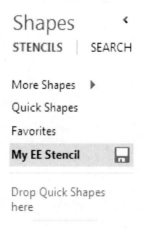

3. Save the stencil.

a) In the **Shapes** window, select the diskette icon next to the stencil name.

b) In the **Save As** dialog box, notice that you are in the **My Shapes** folder.

 Note: By default, Visio saves new stencils in the **My Shapes** folder so that you can easily access them no matter which drawing is open.

c) Select the **File name** field and change **Stencil1.vssx** to *My EE Stencil.vssx*

 Note: Typing the file extension is optional. If you don't add an extension manually, Visio will add an extension automatically based on the option selected in the **Save as type** field.

d) Select **Save**.

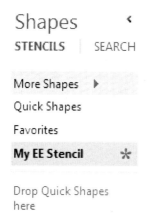

4. Copy the **My EE Logo** shape from the **Favorites** stencil to **My EE Stencil**.

a) In the **Shapes** window, select the **Favorites** stencil.

b) Right-click **My EE Logo**.

c) In the shortcut menu, select **Add to My Shapes→My EE Stencil**.

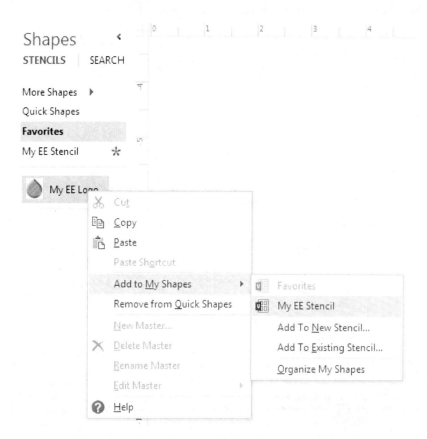

d) In the **Shapes** window, select the **Save Stencil** icon.
   My EE Logo is now a master shape in **My EE Stencil** as well as the **Favorites** stencil.

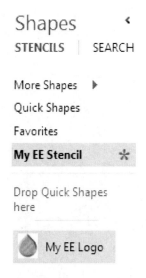

5. Leave this drawing open for the next activity.

TOPIC C

Create Custom Templates

Once you add custom shapes to Visio and organize them into custom stencils, you may want to tie them all together with a custom template. Then, you can use the custom template to create new drawings that contain your custom assets. You can also easily share those assets with others.

Custom Templates

There may be situations when you want to create a custom template. You can do this by saving the open drawing (along with its stencils and master shapes) as a **Visio Template (*.vstx)** file. Unless you specify a different location, Visio will save the template in your **My Documents** or **Documents** folder. Consider saving templates in the **My Shapes** folder so that your custom Visio stencils and templates are in a single location.

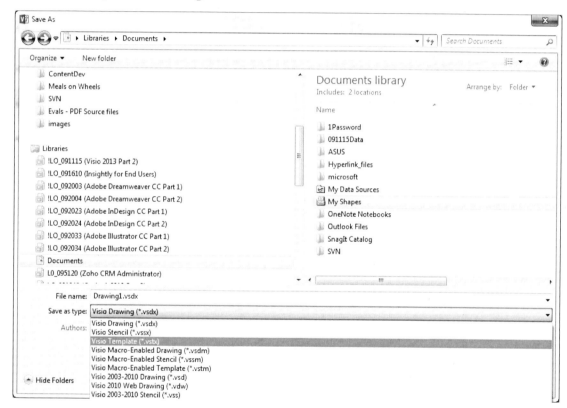

Figure 2-14: Saving a drawing as a custom template.

When to Create a Custom Template

Here are a couple of situations in which you might want to create a custom Visio template:

- You've created a set of stencils and shapes you want to reuse.
- You've created a drawing you want to reuse.

 Access the Checklist tile on your LogicalCHOICE course screen for reference information and job aids on How to Create Custom Templates.

ACTIVITY 2-3
Creating Custom Templates

Before You Begin
The drawing from the last activity is open.

Scenario
Now that you have a custom stencil for Emerald Epicure, you want to create a custom template for the company.

---

1. Save the drawing as a template.

   a) On the ribbon, select the **FILE** tab.
   b) On the **Backstage**, select **Save As**.
   c) On the **Save** screen, verify that **Computer** is selected.

    Computer

   d) Select **Browse**.

   Browse

e) In the **Save As** dialog box, notice that you are in the **Documents** library. Select the **My Shapes** folder.

 Note: By default, Visio saves new templates in the **Documents** library. However, you may want to save templates in the **My Shapes** folder so that you can find them more easily.

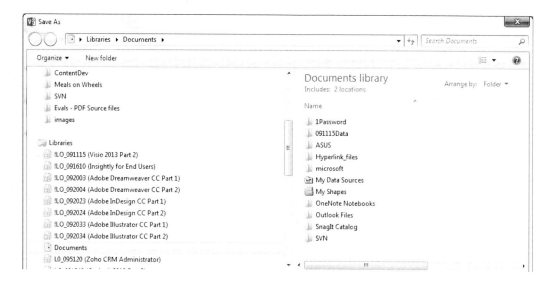

f) In the **Save As** dialog box, select the **Save as type** drop-down field and select the **Visio Template (*.vstx)** option.

g) In the **File name** field, replace Visio's suggested file name with *My EE Template.vstx*

 Note: Typing the file extension is optional. If you don't add an extension manually, Visio will add an extension automatically based on the option selected in the **Save as type** field.

h) Select **Save**.
   Visio closes the **Save As** dialog box.

2. Close Visio.

3. Open Visio but don't select a featured template.

4. Open the template as a new blank drawing.

a) On the Visio start screen, select **CATEGORIES**.

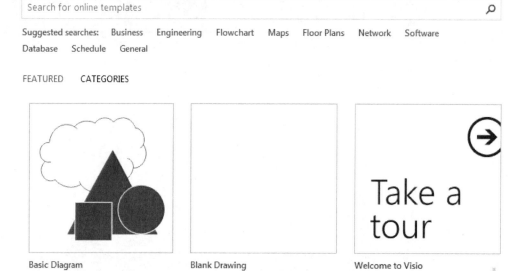

b) In **CATEGORIES**, select the **New from existing** tile.

c) In the **New from existing** preview, select **Create**.

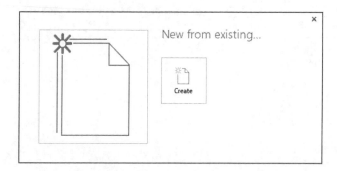

d) In the **New From Existing Drawing** dialog box, notice that you are in the **Documents** library. Select the **My Shapes** folder.

e) Double-click **My EE Template.vstx**.

Visio opens a new drawing based on the custom template, that includes the custom stencil and the custom shape.

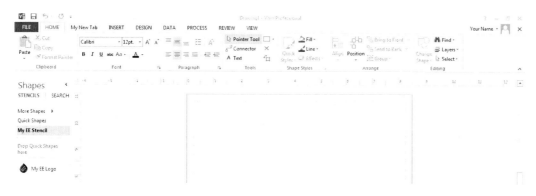

5. Close the drawing without saving it.

6. Close Visio.

Summary

In this lesson, you learned how to create custom shapes, stencils, and templates. You added custom shapes to Visio to produce drawings that reflect the uniqueness of your company. You organized your shapes into custom stencils so that you find and use them when you need them. Finally, you tied all of your assets together with a custom template.

In your work environment, what simple custom shapes do you anticipate adding to a custom Visio stencil?

In your work environment, what Visio drawings would you save as templates so that you can create new drawings based on them?

 Note: Check your LogicalCHOICE Course screen for opportunities to interact with your classmates, peers, and the larger LogicalCHOICE online community about the topics covered in this course or other topics you are interested in. From the Course screen you can also access available resources for a more continuous learning experience.

3 | Connecting Drawings to External Data

Lesson time: 1 hour, 30 minutes

Lesson Objectives

In this lesson, you will connect drawings to external data. You will:

- Make an organization chart from a Microsoft Excel spreadsheet.

- Generate a pivot diagram from an Excel spreadsheet.

- Create a Gantt chart from a Microsoft Project file.

- Create a timeline from a Microsoft Project file.

- Connect a Visio drawing a Microsoft Access database.

Lesson Introduction

You know how to create drawings manually. It can take a lot of time to construct a complex diagram. Visio contains a number of templates, wizards, and tools that will automatically build drawings for you from external data sources.

You can also spend a lot of time keeping your drawings up to date. However, if your drawing is connected to an external data source, you can update the data source and then automatically update the drawing with a single mouse click.

TOPIC A

Make an Organization Chart from an Excel Spreadsheet

Every company has organization charts. Keeping them current can be time consuming. Visio can automatically generate organization charts for you from a Microsoft® Excel® spreadsheet (or other data source).

The Benefits of Linking to External Data

Here are a couple of benefits to linking external data to your Visio drawings:

- You can generate drawings automatically rather than manually.
- You can easily update drawings when the source data changes.

Data Types That Can Be Linked

You can connect a number of data sources to Visio. These include:

- Microsoft Access® databases
- Microsoft Excel spreadsheets
- Microsoft Project plans
- Microsoft SharePoint® lists
- Microsoft SQL Server®
- Object Linking and Embedding Database (OLEDB) databases
- Open Database Connectivity (ODBC) databases

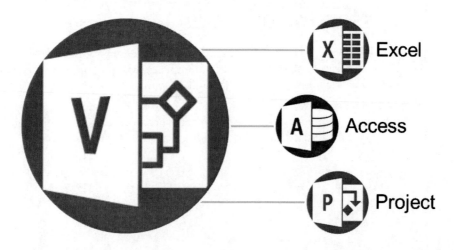

Figure 3-1: Some of the data sources that can be linked to Visio.

The Organization Chart Template

Visio's online library includes an **Organization Chart** template that will automatically create an organization chart from a Microsoft Exchange Server directory, OrgPlus file, or Excel spreadsheet (among others). If you don't see the template on the **FEATURED** tab of the Visio **Start** and **New** screens, you can easily find it by typing *organization* in the template search field.

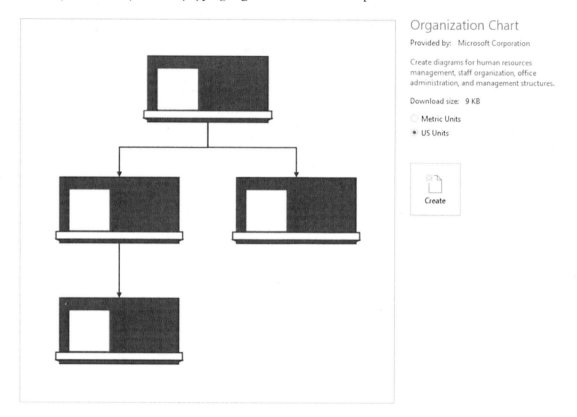

Figure 3-2: A preview of the Organization Chart template.

 Note: OrgPlus is the industry standard software application for automatically creating and distributing organizational charts.

The Organization Chart Wizard

When you choose to create a new drawing by using the **Organization Chart** template, Visio will automatically run the **Organization Chart Wizard**. If you want to create an organization chart from an Excel spreadsheet, the wizard consists of eight screens:

1. Choose whether to create the chart from a data source or manually enter information in the wizard.
2. Indicate the format of the data source.
3. Indicate the location of the data file and the language used.
4. Map the columns in the spreadsheet to the fields in the wizard.
5. Choose which columns of data from the spreadsheet to display in the organization chart.
6. Choose which columns of data from the spreadsheet to add as shape data fields.
7. Indicate the location of photos to import.
8. Choose how you want the chart to be displayed and finish.

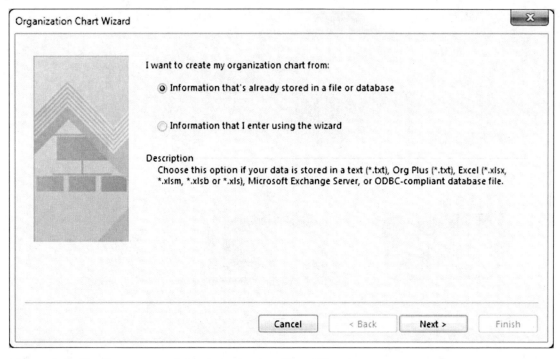

Figure 3-3: The first screen of the Organization Chart Wizard.

If you want the wizard to automatically import photos of each person, you'll need to put all of the photos in a single directory and give each photo a name that matches the first name, last name, or role in the data source.

 Note: The **Organization Chart Wizard** doesn't create a persistent link between the data source and the Visio drawing; it simply uses the data source to construct the chart. So, updating the data source won't update your chart.

Excel Spreadsheet Columns

To accurately build an organization chart for you, the **Organization Chart Wizard** requires your data source to have these four fields:

- **First Name**. This is the first name of each person you want in the chart. The wizard combines this database field with the **Last Name** database field to populate the **Name** field in each organization chart shape.
- **Last Name**. This is the last name of each person you want in the chart. The wizard combines this database field with the **First Name** database field to populate the **Name** field in each organization chart shape.
- **Role**. This is the job title of each person you want in the chart. The wizard uses this database field to populate the **Title** field in each organization chart shape.
- **Reports To**. This is the supervisor of each person you want in the chart. The wizard uses this database field to determine the hierarchical position of each organization chart shape.

If you are using an Excel spreadsheet as the data source for your organization chart, make sure the spreadsheet contains at least four columns that correspond to the four fields. It's okay if the spreadsheet has more than four columns. It's also okay if the column labels in the spreadsheet aren't identical to the labels shown; however, the more similar the labels, the easier it will be for the wizard to match the source fields with the destination fields.

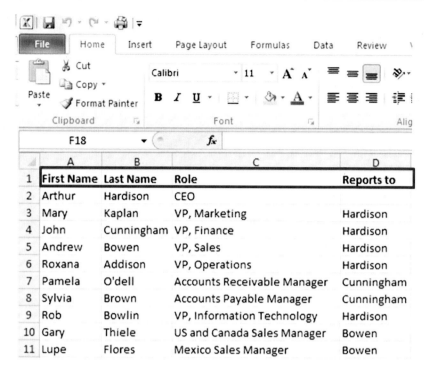

	A	B	C	D
1	First Name	Last Name	Role	Reports to
2	Arthur	Hardison	CEO	
3	Mary	Kaplan	VP, Marketing	Hardison
4	John	Cunningham	VP, Finance	Hardison
5	Andrew	Bowen	VP, Sales	Hardison
6	Roxana	Addison	VP, Operations	Hardison
7	Pamela	O'dell	Accounts Receivable Manager	Cunningham
8	Sylvia	Brown	Accounts Payable Manager	Cunningham
9	Rob	Bowlin	VP, Information Technology	Hardison
10	Gary	Thiele	US and Canada Sales Manager	Bowen
11	Lupe	Flores	Mexico Sales Manager	Bowen

Figure 3-4: The four Excel spreadsheet columns used by the Organization Chart Wizard.

 Access the Checklist tile on your LogicalCHOICE course screen for reference information and job aids on How to Make an Organization Chart from an Excel Spreadsheet.

ACTIVITY 3-1

Making an Organization Chart from an Excel Spreadsheet

Data Files

C:\091115Data\Connecting Drawings to External Data\EE Organization Table.xlsx

C:\091115Data\Connecting Drawings to External Data\Andrew.png

C:\091115Data\Connecting Drawings to External Data\Arthur.png

C:\091115Data\Connecting Drawings to External Data\Gary.png

C:\091115Data\Connecting Drawings to External Data\John.png

C:\091115Data\Connecting Drawings to External Data\Lupe.png

C:\091115Data\Connecting Drawings to External Data\Mary.png

C:\091115Data\Connecting Drawings to External Data\Pamela.png

C:\091115Data\Connecting Drawings to External Data\Rob.png

C:\091115Data\Connecting Drawings to External Data\Roxana.png

C:\091115Data\Connecting Drawings to External Data\Sylvia.png

Before You Begin

Visio is closed.

Scenario

Arthur Hardison, the CEO of Emerald Epicure, asked you to create a manager-level organization chart of the company. Rather than create the chart manually in Visio, you decide to create it from an existing Excel spreadsheet. You also have leadership team photos from the company directory that you want to add automatically to the organization chart.

---

1. Open the Excel spreadsheet.

   a) Open **Windows Explorer**.

   b) Navigate to **C:\091115Data\Connecting Drawings to External Data**.

c) Double-click **EE Organization Table.xlsx**
   The spreadsheet opens in Excel.

	A	B	C	D
1	**First Name**	**Last Name**	**Role**	**Reports to**
2	Arthur	Hardison	CEO	
3	Mary	Kaplan	VP, Marketing	Hardison
4	John	Cunningham	VP, Finance	Hardison
5	Andrew	Bowen	VP, Sales	Hardison
6	Roxana	Addison	VP, Operations	Hardison
7	Pamela	O'dell	Accounts Receivable Manager	Cunningham
8	Sylvia	Brown	Accounts Payable Manager	Cunningham
9	Rob	Bowlin	VP, Information Technology	Hardison
10	Gary	Thiele	US and Canada Sales Manager	Bowen
11	Lupe	Flores	Mexico Sales Manager	Bowen

d) Examine the spreadsheet. Notice the column names.
e) Close Excel.

2. Examine the leadership team photos.

   a) In **Windows Explorer**, notice that the **C:\091115Data\Connecting Drawings to External Data** folder contains 10 *.png files. The file names are the first names of leadership team members.
   b) Double-click **Arthur.png**.
   c) Windows opens the photo of Arthur.

   d) Close Arthur's photo.
   e) View the other photos if you wish.
   f) Minimize **Windows Explorer**.

3. Start a new drawing based on the **Organization Chart** template.

   a) Open Visio.

b) Select the **Organization Chart** template.

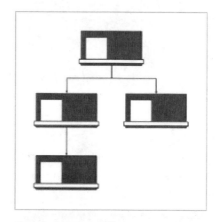

Organization Chart

c) In the **Organization Chart** preview, make sure that the **US Units** radio button is selected.

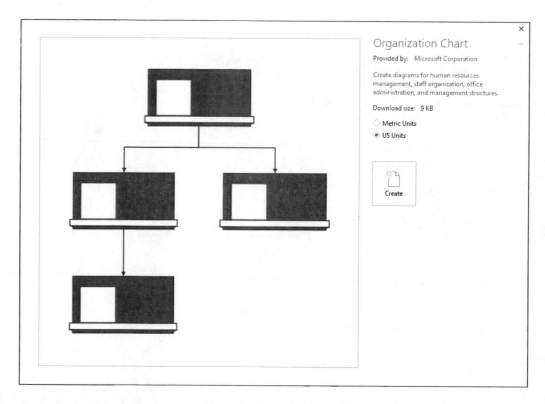

d) Select the **Create** button.
Visio opens a new drawing page and the **Organization Chart Wizard**.

> 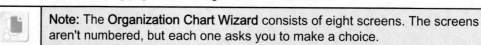 **Note:** The **Organization Chart Wizard** consists of eight screens. The screens aren't numbered, but each one asks you to make a choice.

4. Complete the **I want to create my organization chart from** screen of the **Organization Chart Wizard**.

a) Make sure that the **Information that's already stored in a file or database** radio button is selected.

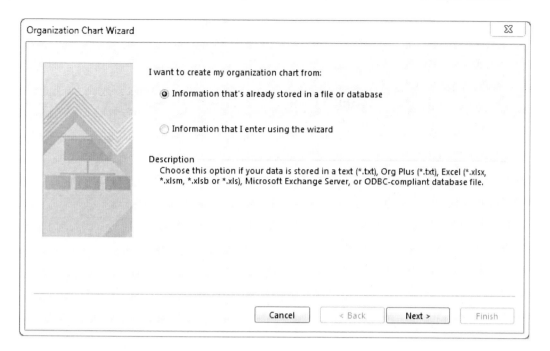

b) Select the **Next** button.

5. Complete the **My organization information is stored in** screen of the **Organization Chart Wizard**.

a) In the **My organization information is stored in** field, select the **A text, Org Plus (*.txt), or Excel file** option.

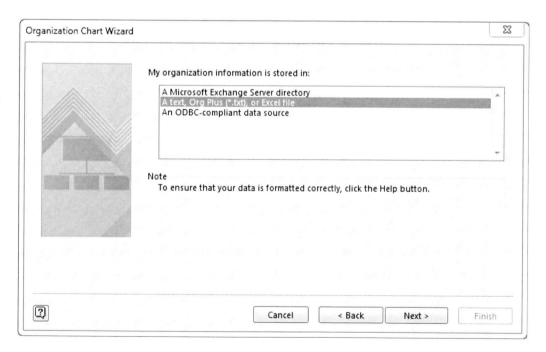

b) Select the **Next** button.

6. Complete the **Locate the file that contains your organization information** screen of the **Organization Chart Wizard**.

a) Select the **Browse** button, navigate to **C:\091115Data\Connecting Drawings to External Data**, and double-click **EE Organization Table.xlsx**.

b) In the **Specify the language** field, make sure that English (United States) is selected.

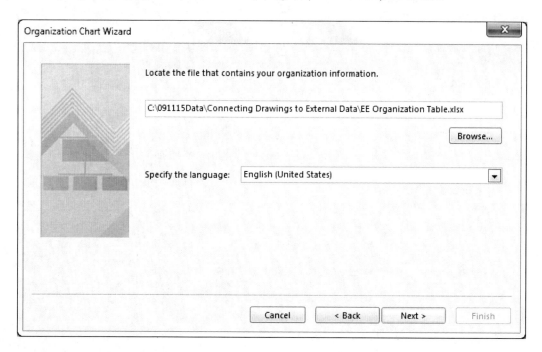

c) Select the **Next** button.

7. Complete the **Choose the columns (fields) in your data file that contain the information that defines the organization** screen of the **Organization Chart Wizard**.

a) Select the **Name** drop-down field and select the **Last Name** option.

b) Make sure that the **Reports to** and **First name** fields are mapped to the same columns in the spreadsheet.

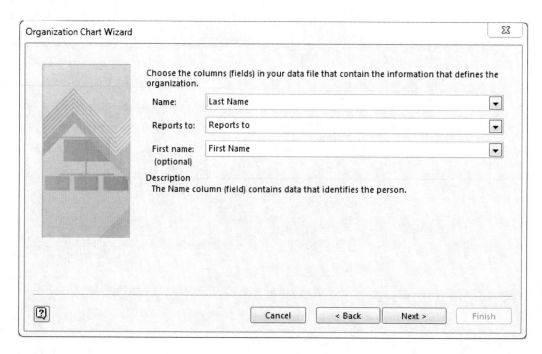

c) Select the **Next** button.

8. Complete the **Choose the columns (fields) from your data file that you want to display** screen of the **Organization Chart Wizard**.

   a) Notice that **Last Name** is already in the **Displayed fields** list.

   b) In the **Data file columns** list, select **Role**.

   c) Select the **Add** button.
      Visio moves **Role** from the **Data file columns** list to the **Displayed fields** list.

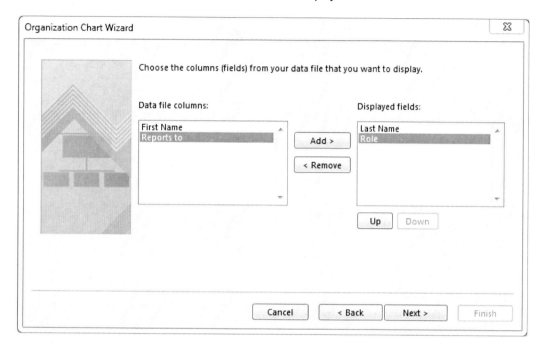

   d) Select the **Next** button.

9. Complete the **Choose the columns (fields) from your data file that you want to add to organization chart shapes as shape data fields** screen of the **Organization Chart Wizard**.

   a) Notice that **Last Name** and **Role** are already in the **Shape Data fields** list.

   b) In the **Data file columns** list, select **Reports to**.

c) Select the **Add** button.
    Visio moves **Reports to** from the **Data file columns** list to the **Shape Data fields** list.

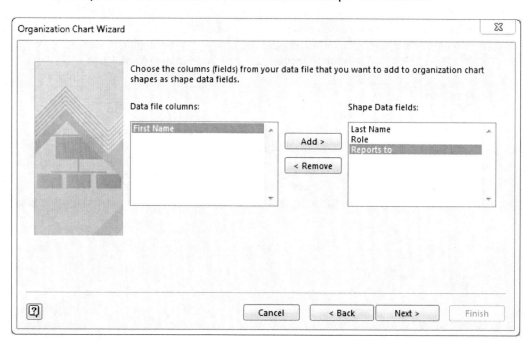

d) Select the **Next** button.

10. Complete the **You can import pictures from your computer or a network location** screen of the **Organization Chart Wizard**.

a) Select the **Locate the folder that contains your organization pictures** radio button.

b) Select the **Browse** button, navigate to **C:\091115Data\Connecting Drawings to External Data**, and select the **Open** button.

c) Select the **Match pictures based on** drop-down field and select the **First Name** option.

d) Select the **Next** button.

11. Complete the **Your organization data may contain too many employees to fit on one page of your drawing** screen of the **Organization Chart Wizard**.

   a) Make sure that the **I want the wizard to automatically break my organization chart across pages** radio button is selected.

   b) Select the **Name at top of page** drop-down field and select **Arthur Hardison**.

   c) Verify that both check boxes are checked.

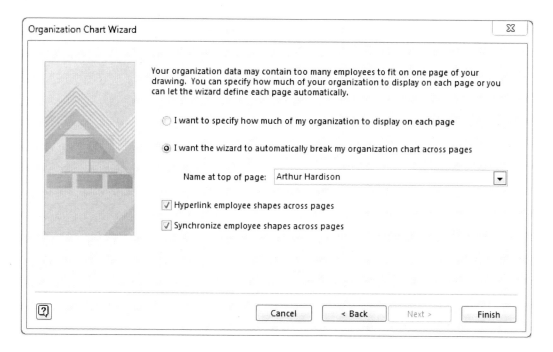

   d) Select the **Finish** button.

      Visio builds the organization chart based on the Excel spreadsheet and automatically adds photos.

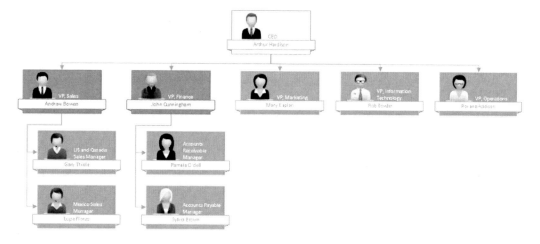

12. Save the organization chart.

   a) On the ribbon, select the **FILE** tab.

   b) On the **Backstage**, select **Save As**.

   c) On the **Save As** screen, make sure that **Computer** is selected.

   d) Select the **Browse** button.

   e) In the **Save As** dialog box, navigate to **C:\091115Data\Connecting Drawings to External Data**.

f)   In the **File name** filed, type *My EE Organization Chart.vsdx*

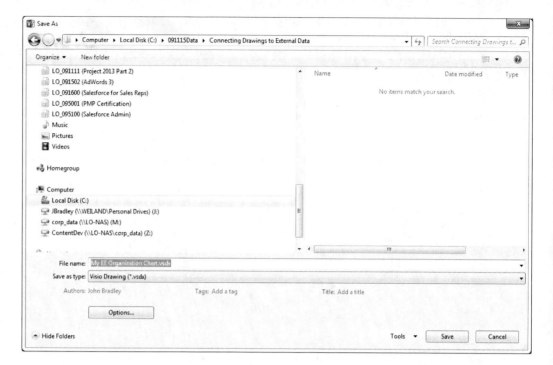

g)   Select the **Save** button.

13. Close Visio.

TOPIC B

Generate a Pivot Diagram from an Excel Spreadsheet

A pivot diagram is another type of drawing that Visio can automatically generate for you from an Excel spreadsheet. If your company uses pivot tables and pivot charts, knowing how to generate and modify a pivot diagram is a valuable skill.

PivotDiagrams

A *pivot table* is a data summarization tool found in data visualization programs such as spreadsheets or business intelligence software. Microsoft Excel refers to this feature as a PivotTable. Among other functions, a pivot table can automatically categorize, sort, count, total, and average the data stored in another table or spreadsheet.

A *pivot chart* is a graphical representation of a pivot table. In Microsoft Excel, this feature is referred to as a PivotChart. In Microsoft Visio, a pivot chart is referred to as a either a *pivot diagram* or a PivotDiagram.

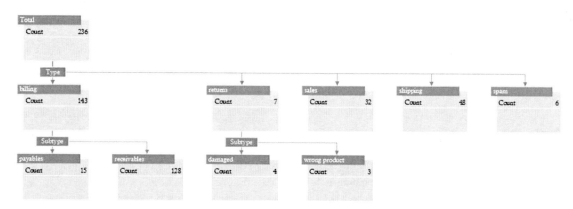

Figure 3-5: A PivotDiagram in Visio.

A pivot diagram looks a lot like an organization chart—with information arranged in a hierarchy. The top level represents the entire data set. Lower levels represent increasingly finer levels of detail. Each box in the diagram is referred to as a node. Individual nodes can be expanded or collapsed to focus on data of interest.

The Pivot Diagram Template

Visio's online library includes a **Pivot Diagram** template that will automatically create a pivot diagram from an Excel spreadsheet or other data source. If you don't see the template on the **FEATURED** tab of the Visio **Start** and **New** screens, you can easily find it by typing *pivot* in the template search field.

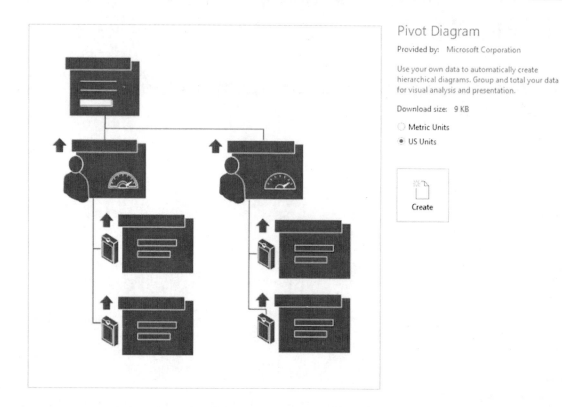

Pivot Diagram

Provided by: Microsoft Corporation

Use your own data to automatically create hierarchical diagrams. Group and total your data for visual analysis and presentation.

Download size: 9 KB

○ Metric Units
● US Units

Create

Figure 3-6: A preview of the Pivot Diagram template.

The primary advantage of creating a **Pivot Diagram** in Visio, rather than using the **PivotChart** in Excel, is that Visio allows you more flexibility in changing the look of the chart.

The Data Selector Tool

When you choose to use the **Pivot Diagram** template to create a new drawing, Visio will automatically run the **Data Selector** dialog box. This is an generic tool that can be used to connect many drawing types to external data. If you want to create a pivot diagram from an Excel spreadsheet, the **Data Selector** consists of five screens:

1. What data do you want to use?
2. What workbook do you want to import?
3. What worksheet do you want to use?
4. Which column and rows do you want to include?
5. Finish.

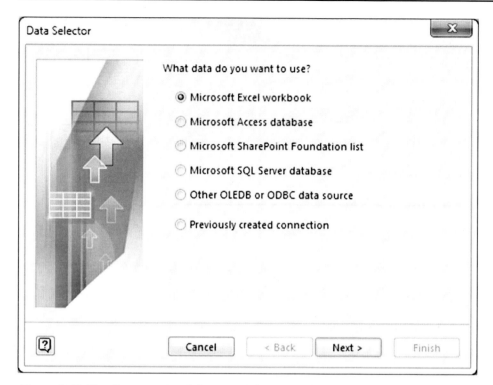

Figure 3-7: The first screen of the Data Selector tool.

 Note: Unlike the **Organization Chart Wizard**, the **Data Selector** creates a persistent link between the data source and the Visio drawing. So, you can update your data source and then easily update your chart.

The PIVOT DIAGRAM Tab

After you complete the five screens of the **Data Selector** tool, Visio will generate a pivot diagram from the source data. Visio will also open the **PIVOT DIAGRAM** tab—which consists of a number of commands for modifying your pivot diagram.

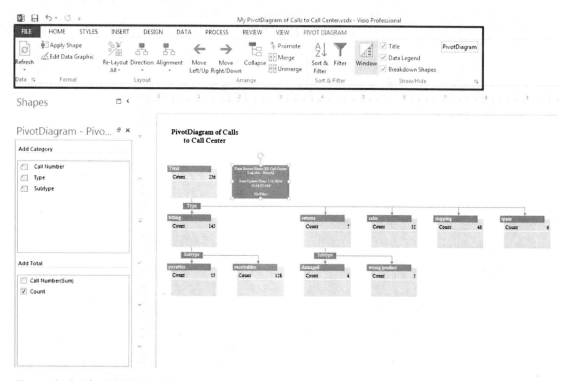

Figure 3-8: The PIVOT DIAGRAM tab.

The following table briefly explains how you can use each command.

Command	Use
Refresh	Update the pivot diagram after making a change to the data source.
Apply Shape	Add a shape to the selected node or change the applied shape.
Edit Data Graphic	Change the data properties of the selected node.
Re-Layout All	Rearrange the diagram so that it is easier to read.
Direction	Change how levels of detail are presented. The options are: • **Top-to-Bottom** (default) • **Bottom-to-Top** • **Left-to-Right** • **Right-to-Left**
Alignment	Change how nodes are aligned with one another. The options are: • **Left** (default) • **Center** • **Right** • **Top** • **Middle** • **Bottom**
Move Left/Up	Move a node left or up in the same level.
Move Right/Down	Move a node right or down in the same level.
Collapse	Hide child nodes of the selected node.
Promote	Move a node to a higher level.
Merge	Combine two or more nodes into a single node.

Command	Use
Unmerge	Separate a combined node into individual notes.
Sort & Filter	Change the order of nodes in a level based on specified criteria.
Filter	Change which data is displayed based on specified criteria.
Window	Show or hide the PivotDiagram window (to be discussed later in this topic).
Title	Show or hide the title shape.
Data Legend	Show or hide the data legend shape.
Breakdown Shapes	Show or hide breakdown shapes between parent and child nodes.

The PivotDiagram Window

When Visio generates a pivot diagram from source data, it opens the **Pivot Diagram** window on the left side of the screen and moves the **Shapes** window to the bottom left corner. The **PivotDiagram** window has two sections:

- **Add Category**—which lists the column in the data source. Select a column name to add a level of detail to the pivot diagram.
- **Add Total**—which lists the ways that the source data can be totaled. Check a check box to display totals using that method. Uncheck a check box to hide totals using that method.

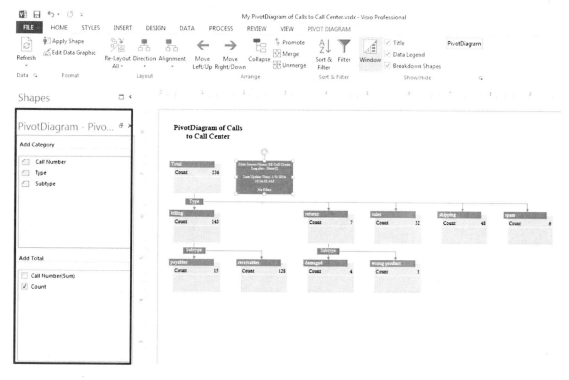

Figure 3-9: The PivotDiagram window.

 Access the Checklist tile on your LogicalCHOICE course screen for reference information and job aids on How to Generate a Pivot Diagram from an Excel Spreadsheet.

ACTIVITY 3-2

Generating a PivotDiagram from an Excel Spreadsheet

Data File

C:\091115Data\Connecting Drawings to External Data\EE Call Center Log.xlsx

Before You Begin

Visio is closed.

Scenario

Emerald Epicure call center employees are required to log each incoming phone by type and subtype. Every month, EE's customer relationship management system generates an Excel spreadsheet containing this data. Roxana Addison, the vice president of operations, provided you with the spreadsheet from last month and asked you to create a PivotDiagram depicting the data.

---

1. Open the Excel spreadsheet.
   a) Maximize **Windows Explorer**.
   b) Navigate to **C:\091115Data\Connecting Drawings to External Data**.

c) Double-click **EE Call Center Log.xlsx**
The spreadsheet opens in Excel.

	A	B	C
1	**Call Number**	**Type**	**Subtype**
2	1	billing	receivables
3	2	shipping	express
4	3	billing	receivables
5	4	billing	payables
6	5	shipping	express
7	6	sales	Canada
8	7	shipping	express
9	8	sales	Canada
10	9	sales	Canada
11	10	billing	receivables
12	11	billing	receivables
13	12	billing	receivables
14	13	billing	receivables
15	14	sales	Canada
16	15	shipping	express
17	16	billing	receivables
18	17	shipping	express
19	18	billing	receivables
20	19	spam	
21	20	sales	Canada
22	21	billing	receivables
23	22	returns	damaged
24	23	billing	receivables
25	24	billing	receivables

d) Examine the spreadsheet. Notice the column names.
e) Close Excel.
f) Minimize **Windows Explorer**.

2. Start a new drawing based on the **PivotDiagram** template.
a) Open Visio.
b) On the Visio **Start** screen, in the **Search for online templates** field, type *pivot* and select the
magnifying class icon. 🔍

c) Select the **PivotDiagram** template.

Pivot Diagram

d) In the **PivotDiagram** preview, verify that the **US Units** radio button is selected.

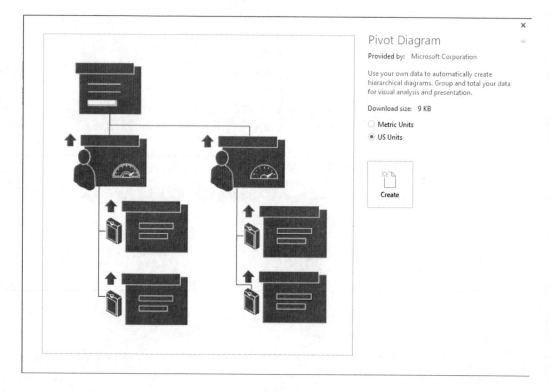

e) Select the **Create** button.
Visio opens a new drawing page and the **Data Selector**.

3. Generate a PivotDiagram by using the **Data Selector**.

a) In the **Data Selector**, verify that the **Microsoft Excel workbook** radio button is selected.

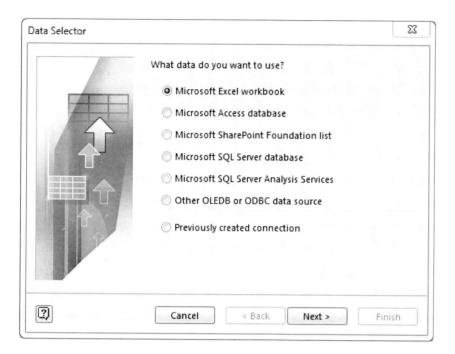

b) Select the **Next** button.
c) Select the **Browse** button.
d) Navigate to **C:\091115Data\Connecting Drawings to External Data** and double-click **EE Call Center Log.xlsx**.

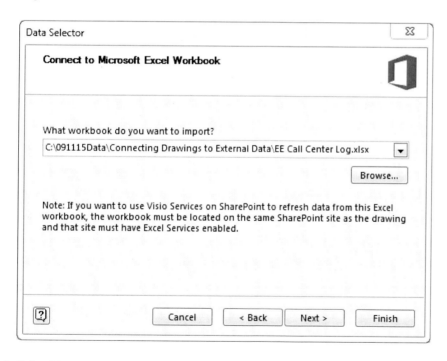

e) Select **Next**.

f) Review the next screen of the **Data Selector**.

This Excel file consists of a single worksheet, so no changes are needed.

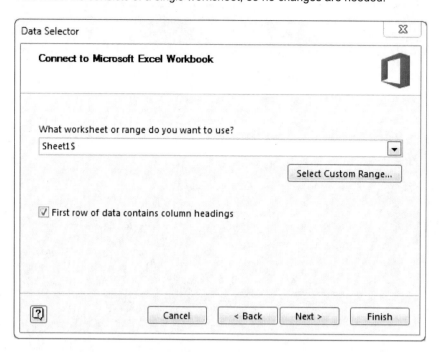

g) Select **Next**.

h) Review the next screen of the **Data Selector**.

You want to use all columns and rows on the worksheet, so no changes are needed.

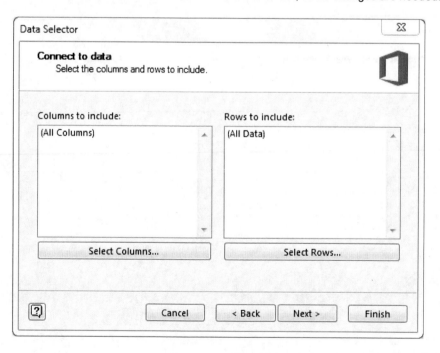

i) Select **Next**.
The **Data Selector** says that you successfully imported your data.

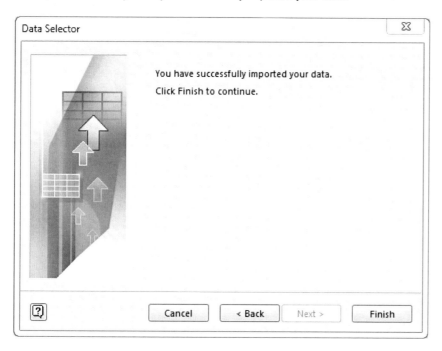

j) Select **Finish**.
Visio creates a collapsed PivotDiagram and opens the **PivotDiagram** window to the left of the drawing page. (The **Shapes** window is in the bottom left corner.) Visio also adds a **PIVOT DIAGRAM** tab on the ribbon.

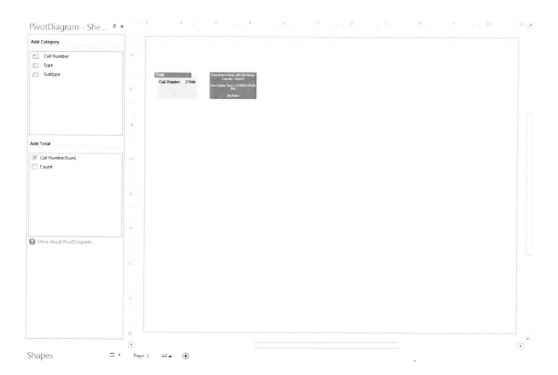

 Note: If the text is too small to read on your screen, you can increase the size of the text and shapes by using the **Zoom** tool in the **Status Bar**.

4. Change the totaling method.

   a) In the **Total** shape, notice that Visio displays the sum of the **Call Number** field, which isn't meaningful information.

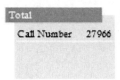

   b) In the **PivotDiagram** window, in the **Add Total** section, uncheck the **Call Number(Sum)** check box and check the **Count** check box.

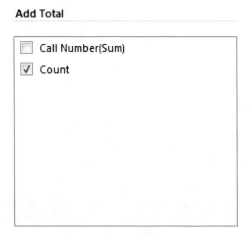

   c) Notice that the **Total** shape now displays a count of the number of calls received, which is meaningful information.

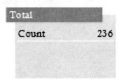

5. Add categories to the **PivotDiagram**.

   a) Verify that the **Total** shape is selected.

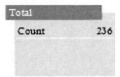

b) In the **PivotDiagram** window, in the **Add Category** section, select **Type**.
Visio adds a new level of shapes showing the number of each type of call.

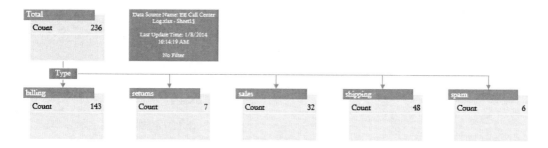

c) Verify that the **billing**, **returns**, **sales**, **shipping**, and **spam** shapes are selected.
d) In the **PivotDiagram** window, in the **Add Category** section, select **Subtype**.
Visio adds another new level of shapes showing the number of each subtype of call.

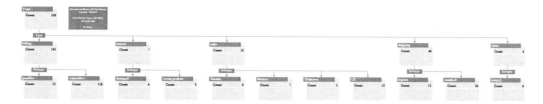

6. Change the theme so that you can see the **Title** shape.

Above the **Total** shape is a **Title** shape containing the text **Sheet1$**. However, because the text color is light grey, you may not be able to see it on your monitor.

a) On the ribbon, select the **DESIGN** tab.
b) In the **Themes** group, select the **Simple** theme, the fifth option from the left.

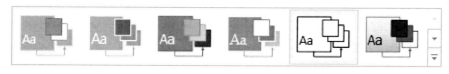

Themes

c) Notice the **Title** shape.

The **Sheet1$** text in the **Title** shape is the name of the worksheet in the Excel spreadsheet used to generate the PivotDiagram. You should change the title to something more meaningful.

Sheet1$

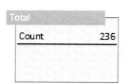

7. Change the **Title** and hide the **Data Legend**.

a) Select the **Title** shape.
b) On the ribbon, select the **PIVOT DIAGRAM** tab.

c) In the **Show/Hide** group, select the **Data Options** icon.

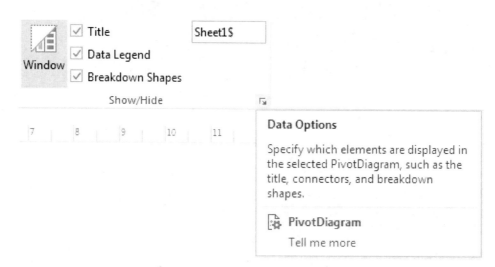

d) In the **PivotDiagram Options** dialog box, verify that the **Title** text field is selected, and replace the text Sheet1$ with *PivotDiagram of Calls to Call Center*

e) In the **Diagram Options** section, uncheck the **Show data legend** check box.

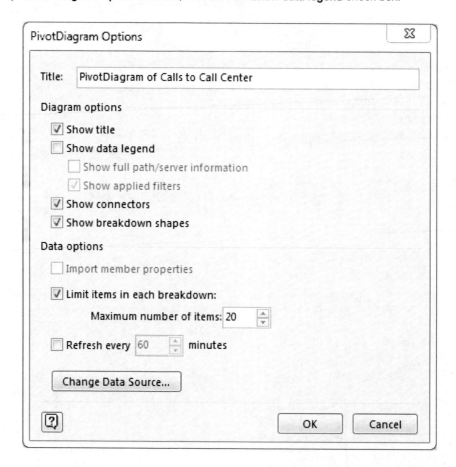

f)   Select **OK** to close the dialog box.
     Notice that the **Title** is changed and the **Data Legend** is hidden.

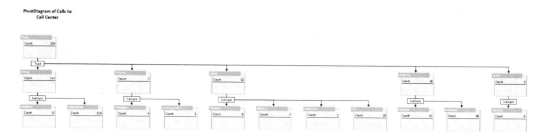

8. Save the file in the **C:\091115Data\Connecting Drawings to External Data** folder as *My PivotDiagram of Calls to Call Center.vsdx*

9. Close Visio.

TOPIC C

Create a Gantt Chart from a Project File

Does your company use Microsoft Project to manage its projects? If so, you'll be glad to know that Visio can automatically create Gantt charts from your Project files. This means you don't have to spend valuable time manually building and maintaining Gantt charts.

Microsoft Project

A *project* is a temporary initiative to create a unique result. *Project management* is the administration and supervision of projects by using a well-defined set of knowledge, skills, tools, and techniques. Microsoft Project Professional 2013 is a powerful tool for managing projects so that they are completed on time, within budget, and according to specifications.

Figure 3-10: The Microsoft Project Start screen.

Gantt Charts

Microsoft Project can display project information in a number of ways. The default (and most commonly used) view is the *Gantt chart*. A Gantt chart has two sections. In the left-hand section, project tasks and information about those task is shown in rows and columns (much like a spreadsheet). In the right-hand section, the duration of each task is plotted as a bar against the dates along the top of the section.

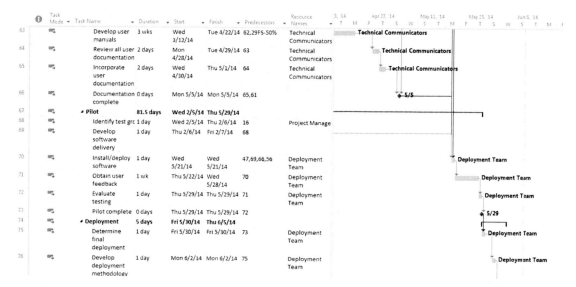

Figure 3-11: A Gantt chart created in Microsoft Project.

 Note: The Gantt chart is named after Henry Gantt, who designed this tool between 1910 and 1915. Although now regarded as a common charting technique, Gantt charts were considered revolutionary when first introduced.

The Gantt Chart Template

Visio's online library includes a Gantt chart template that enables you to import information from a Microsoft Project file and construct a Gantt chart drawing. If you don't see the template on the **FEATURED** tab of the Visio **Start** and **New** screens, you can easily find it by typing *gantt* in the template search field.

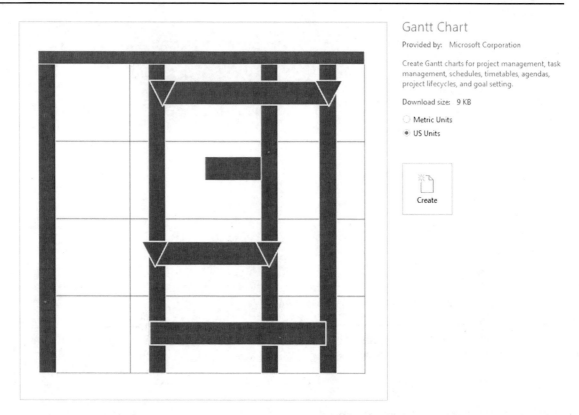

Figure 3-12: Creating a new drawing with the Gantt chart template.

The primary advantage of creating a Gantt chart in Visio, rather than using the **Gantt Chart** view in Project, is that Visio allows you more flexibility in changing the look of the chart.

Gantt Chart Options

When you choose to use the **Gantt Chart** template to create a new drawing, Visio will automatically run the **Gantt Chart Options** dialog box. This dialog box is designed to help you build a Gantt chart from scratch. If you plan to generate the Gantt chart from a Project file, simply close the dialog box by selecting the **Cancel** button.

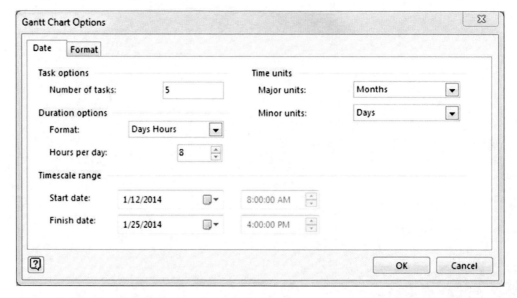

Figure 3-13: The Gantt Chart options dialog box.

The Import Project Data Wizard

Instead of using the **Gantt Chart Options** dialog box to build a Gantt chart in Visio, you can use the **Import Project Data Wizard**. You can run this wizard by navigating to the **GANTT CHART** tab (which will be discussed later in this topic) and selecting the **Import Data** command. If you want to create a Gantt chart from a Project file, this wizard has six screens:

1. Choose whether to create the Gantt chart from a Project file (or other data source) or manually enter information in the wizard.
2. Indicate the format of the data source.
3. Indicate the location of the data file.
4. Select the time scale.
5. Select which task types to include.
6. Finish.

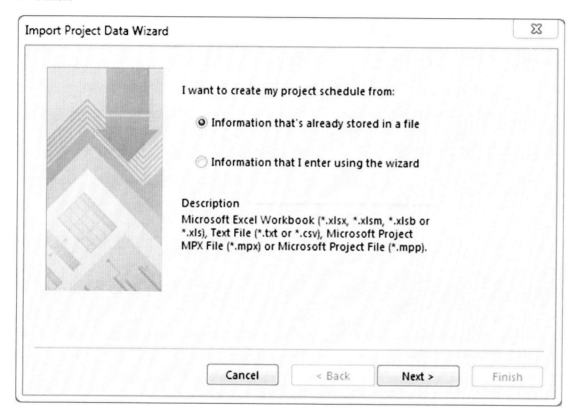

Figure 3-14: The first screen of the Import Project Data Wizard.

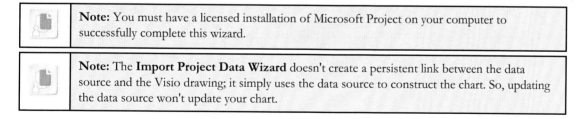

Note: You must have a licensed installation of Microsoft Project on your computer to successfully complete this wizard.

Note: The **Import Project Data Wizard** doesn't create a persistent link between the data source and the Visio drawing; it simply uses the data source to construct the chart. So, updating the data source won't update your chart.

The Gantt Chart Tab

After you create a new drawing by using the **Gantt Chart** template, Visio will also open the **GANTT CHART** tab—which consists of a number of commands for creating and modifying your Gantt chart.

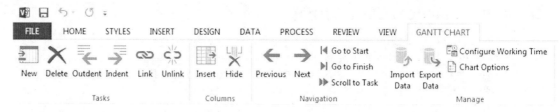

Figure 3-15: The GANTT CHART tab.

This table briefly how you can use each command.

Command	Use
New	Insert a new task above the selected task.
Delete	Remove the selected task.
Outdent	Outdent the selected task to the left.
Indent	Indent the selected task to the right.
Link	Create dependencies between two or more selected tasks.
Unlink	Remove dependencies between two or more selected tasks.
Insert	Insert a new data column to the right of the selected data column.
Hide	Hide the selected data column.
Previous	Go to the task before the selected task on the timeline.
Next	Go to the task after the selected task on the timeline.
Go to Start	Go to the first task on the timeline.
Go to Finish	Go to the last task on the timeline.
Scroll to Task	Go to the selected task.
Import Data	Open the **Import Project Data Wizard**.
Export Data	Open the **Export Project Data Wizard** and export the data in Microsoft Project or Microsoft Excel formats (among others).
Configure Working Time	Change the days of the week and hours of the day when work is performed on the project.
Chart Option	Open the **Gantt Chart Options** dialog box.

 Access the Checklist tile on your LogicalCHOICE course screen for reference information and job aids on How to Create a Gantt Chart from a Project File.

ACTIVITY 3-3
Creating a Gantt Chart from a Project File

Data File

C:\091115Data\Connecting Drawings to External Data\Cinnamon Oil Project.mpp

Before You Begin

Visio is closed.

Scenario

The senior management team at Emerald Epicure is considering a project to add cinnamon oil to the company's product line. Arther Hardison, the CEO, has created a project plan in Microsoft Project. He has asked you to use this file to create a visually attractive Gantt chart.

---

1. Open the Project file.
   a) Maximize **Windows Explorer**.
   b) Navigate to **C:\091115Data\Connecting Drawings to External Data**.
   c) Double-click **Cinnamon Oil Project.mpp**.
      A Gantt chart opens in Project.

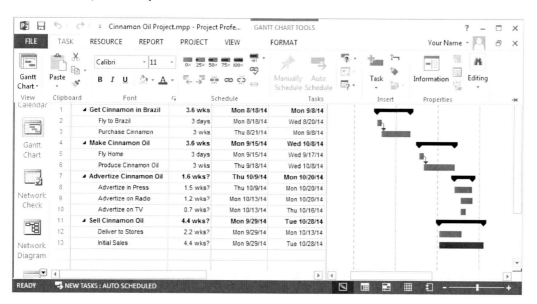

   d) Examine the Gantt chart. Notice the task information in the left pane and the task bars in the right pane.
   e) Close Project.
   f) Minimize **Windows Explorer**.

2. Start a new drawing based on the **Gantt Chart** template.
   a) Open Visio.
   b) On the Visio **Start** screen, in the **Search for online templates** field, type *gantt* and select the magnifying class icon. 🔍

c) Select the **Gantt Chart** template.

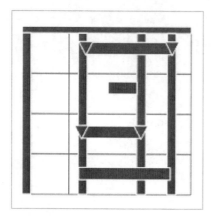

Gantt Chart

d) In the **Gantt Chart** preview, verify that the **US Units** radio button is selected.

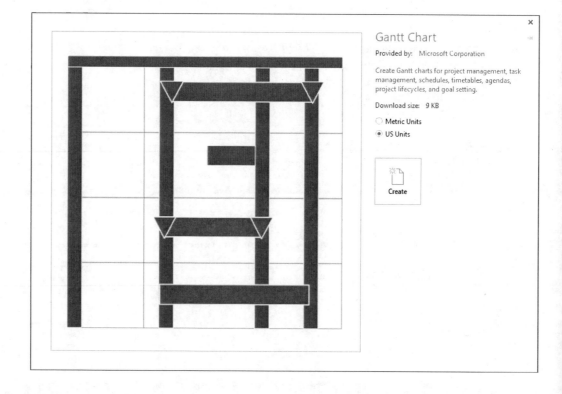

e) Select the **Create** button.
   Visio opens a new drawing page and the **Gantt Chart Options** dialog box.

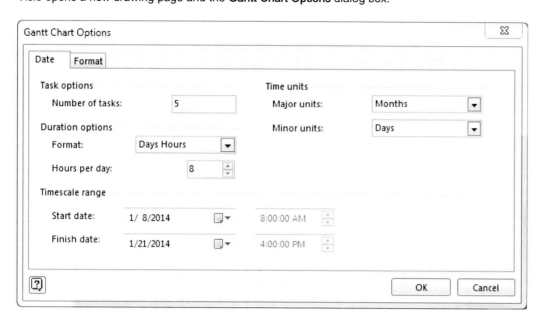

f) Select the **Cancel** button.

3. Use the **Import Project Data Wizard** to create a Gantt chart.

   a) On the ribbon, select the **GANTT CHART** tab.
   b) In the **Manage** group, select the **Import Data** command.
   c) In the **Import Project Data Wizard**, verify that the **Information that's already stored in a file** radio
      button is selected.

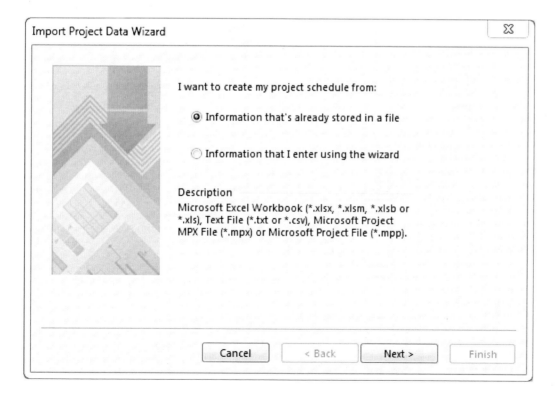

   d) Select the **Next** button.

e) In the **Select the format of your project data** field, verify that **Microsoft Project File** is selected.

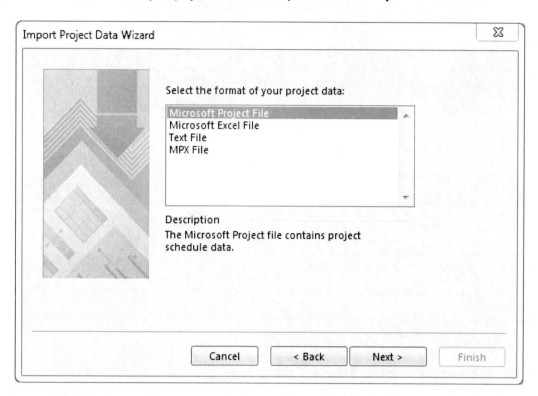

f) Select the **Next** button.

g) On the next screen, select the **Browse** button, navigate to **C:\091115Data\Connecting Drawings to External Data** and double-click **Cinnamon Oil Project.mpp.**

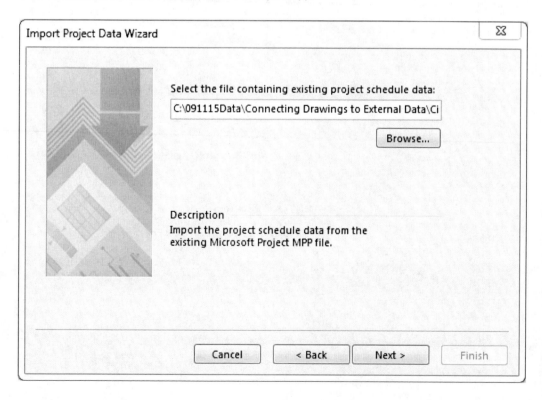

h) Select the **Next** button.

i) On the next screen, review the **Time scale** and **Duration options** but don't make any changes.

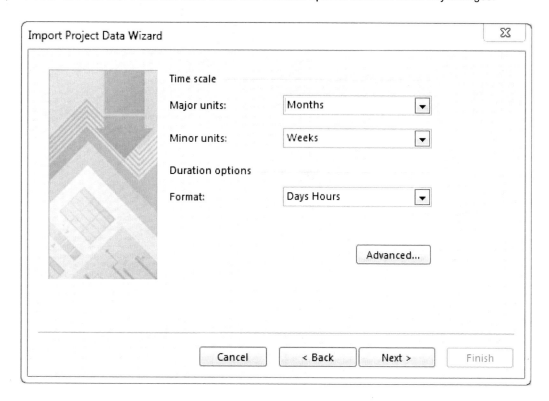

j) Select the **Next** button.
k) In the **Select task types to include** field, verify that **All** is selected.

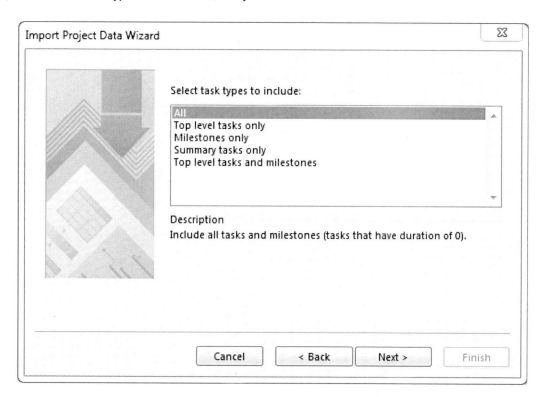

l) Select the **Next** button.

m) On the next screen, review the import properties.

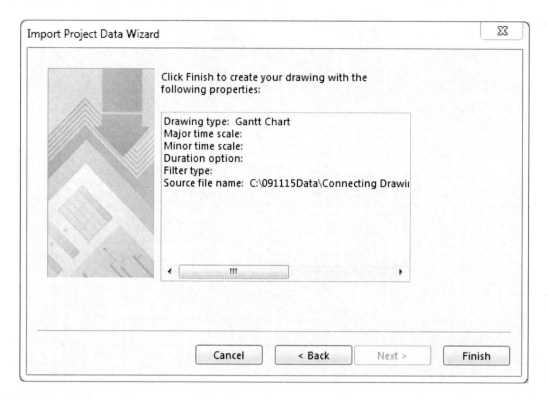

n) Select the **Finish** button.
   Visio builds a Gantt chart from the Project file.

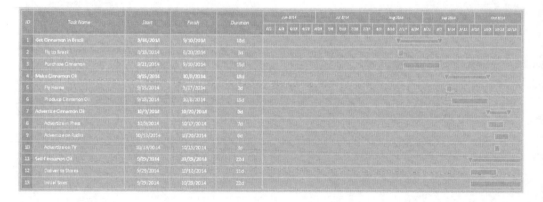

4. Change the **Theme**.
   a) On the ribbon, select the **DESIGN** tab.
   b) In the **Themes** group, select the **Simple** theme, the fifth option from the left.

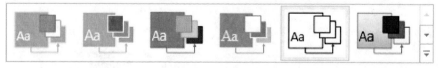

Themes

c) Notice that the Gantt chart now has better color contrast..

ID	Task Name	Start	Finish	Duration	Aug 2014				Sep 2014				Oct 2014			
					8/3	8/10	8/17	8/24	8/31	9/7	9/14	9/21	9/28	10/5	10/12	10/19
1	Get Cinnamon in Brazil	8/18/2014	9/10/2014	18d												
2	Fly to Brazil	8/18/2014	8/20/2014	3d												
3	Purchase Cinnamon	8/21/2014	9/10/2014	15d												
4	Make Cinnamon Oil	9/15/2014	10/8/2014	18d												
5	Fly Home	9/15/2014	9/17/2014	3d												
6	Produce Cinnamon Oil	9/18/2014		15d												
7	Advertize Cinnamon Oil	10/9/2014	10/20/2014	8d												
8	Advertize in Press	10/9/2014	10/17/2014	7d												
9	Advertize on Radio	10/13/2014	10/20/2014	6d												
10	Advertize on TV	10/13/2014	10/15/2014	3d												
11	Sell Cinnamon Oil	9/29/2014	10/28/2014	22d												
12	Deliver to Stores	9/29/2014	10/13/2014	11d												
13	Initial Sales	9/29/2014	10/28/2014	22d												

5. Increase the font size.

   a) Press the **Ctrl** and **A** keys to select all shapes in the drawing.

   b) On the ribbon, select the **HOME** tab.

   c) In the **Font** group, select the **Increase Font Size** icon A a couple of times until the font size is 18pt.

ID	Task Name	Start	Finish	Duration	Aug 2014				Sep 2014				Oct 2014
					8/3	8/10	8/17	8/24	8/31	9/7	9/14	9/21	9/28	10/5
1	Get Cinnamon in Brazil	8/18/2014	9/10/2014	18d									
2	Fly to Brazil	8/18/2014	8/20/2014	3d									
3	Purchase Cinnamon	8/21/2014	9/10/2014	15d									
4	Make Cinnamon Oil	9/15/2014	10/8/2014	18d									
5	Fly Home	9/15/2014	9/17/2014	3d									
6	Produce Cinnamon Oil	9/18/2014		15d									
7	Advertize Cinnamon Oil	10/9/2014	10/20/2014	8d									
8	Advertize in Press	10/9/2014	10/17/2014	7d									
9	Advertize on Radio	10/13/2014	10/20/2014	6d									
10	Advertize on TV	10/13/2014	10/15/2014	3d									
11	Sell Cinnamon Oil	9/29/2014	10/28/2014	22d									
12	Deliver to Stores	9/29/2014	10/13/2014	11d									
13	Initial Sales	9/29/2014	10/28/2014	22d									

6. Resize the chart.

   a) Press the **Esc** key to deselect all shapes in the drawing.

   b) Select the right border of the Gantt chart, which selects the Gantt chart as a whole.

c) Grab the **Resize Shape** handle on the middle right side of the chart.

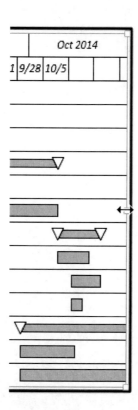

d) Drag the right side of the chart about a half inch to the right until the ends of the last three task bars are no longer truncated.

iD	Task Name	Start	Finish	Duration	Aug 2014					Sep 2014				Oct 2014	
					8/3	8/10	8/17	8/24	8/31	9/7	9/14	9/21	9/28	10/5	
1	**Get Cinnamon in Brazil**	**8/18/2014**	**9/10/2014**	**18d**											
2	Fly to Brazil	8/18/2014	8/20/2014	3d											
3	Purchase Cinnamon	8/21/2014	9/10/2014	15d											
4	**Make Cinnamon Oil**	**9/15/2014**	**10/8/2014**	**18d**											
5	Fly Home	9/15/2014	9/17/2014	3d											
6	Produce Cinnamon Oil	9/18/2014		15d											
7	**Advertize Cinnamon Oil**	**10/9/2014**	**10/20/2014**	**8d**											
8	Advertize in Press	10/9/2014	10/17/2014	7d											
9	Advertize on Radio	10/13/2014	10/20/2014	6d											
10	Advertize on TV	10/13/2014	10/15/2014	3d											
11	**Sell Cinnamon Oil**	**9/29/2014**	**10/28/2014**	**22d**											
12	Deliver to Stores	9/29/2014	10/13/2014	11d											
13	Initial Sales	9/29/2014	10/28/2014	22d											

7. Save the file in the **C:\091115Data\Connecting Drawings to External Data** folder as *My Cinnamon Oil Project Gantt Chart.vsdx*

8. Close Visio.

TOPIC D

Create a Timeline from a Project File

If you company uses Microsoft Project to manage its projects, you'll also be glad to know that Visio can automatically create timelines from your Project files. Again, this means you don't have to spend valuable time manually building and maintaining timelines.

Timelines

In Microsoft Project, a timeline is a snapshot of a project's key tasks and milestones. This is a new feature in Project 2013. It enables project managers to quickly and easily capture the big picture and share it with project sponsors, stakeholders, and team members. Project managers can copy the timeline and paste it in an Outlook email message, a PowerPoint slide, or Word document.

Figure 3-16: A timeline created in Microsoft Project.

The Timeline Template

Visio's online library includes a **Timeline** template that enables you to import information from a Microsoft Project file and construct a timeline drawing. If you don't see the template on the **FEATURED** tab of the Visio **Start** and **New** screens, you can easily find it by typing *timeline* in the template search field.

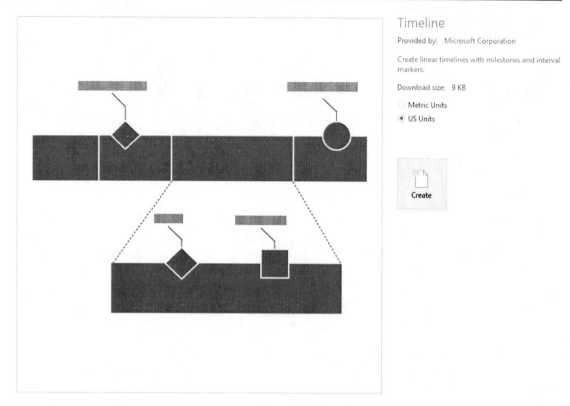

Figure 3-17: Creating a new drawing with the Timeline template.

The primary advantage of creating a **Timeline** in Visio, rather than using the **Timeline** view in Project, is that Visio allows you more flexibility in changing the look of the timeline.

The TIMELINE Tab

After you create a new drawing by using the **Timeline** template, Visio will also open the **TIMELINE** tab—which consists of a number of commands for creating and modifying your Gantt chart.

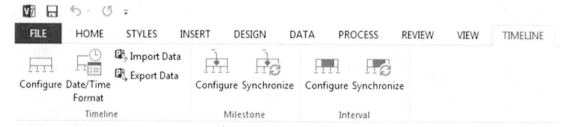

Figure 3-18: The TIMELINE tab.

The following table briefly explains how you can use each command.

Command	Use
Configure	Change the **Time Period** and **Time Format** settings
Date/Time Format	Change how dates and time are displayed.
Import Data	Open the **Import Time Wizard** and create a new timeline from a Microsoft Project file.
Export Data	Export the timeline to a Microsoft Project file.

Command	Use
Milestone | Configure	Change how milestones are displayed.
Milestone | Synchronize	Synchronize milestones that are shared on more than one page.
Interval | Configure	Change how time periods are displayed.
Interval | Synchronize	Synchronize time periods that are shared on more than one page.

The Import Timeline Wizard

The **Import Timeline Wizard** doesn't start automatically when you use the Timeline wizard to create a new drawing. You can manually run this wizard by navigating to the **TIMELINE** tab and selecting the **Import Data** command. This wizard has four screens:

1. Select a Microsoft Project file to import.
2. Select the task levels to include.
3. Select shapes for the timeline.
4. Finish.

Figure 3-19: The first screen of the Import Timeline Wizard.

 Note: You must have a licensed installation of Microsoft Project on your computer to successfully complete this wizard.

Note: The **Import Timeline Wizard** doesn't create a persistent link between the data source and the Visio drawing; it simply uses the data source to construct the timeline. So, updating the data source won't update your timeline.

 Access the Checklist tile on your LogicalCHOICE course screen for reference information and job aids on How to Create a Timeline from a Project File.

ACTIVITY 3-4
Creating a Timeline from a Project File

Data File

C:\091115Data\Connecting Drawings to External Data\Cinnamon Oil Project Milestones.mpp

Before You Begin

Visio is closed.

Scenario

Arther Hardison is pleased with the Gantt chart you created for the Cinnamon Oil Project. While you were building it, he added project milestones to his Microsoft Project file. He has asked you to create a visually attractive timeline of the project milestones.

---

1. Open the Project file.
   a) Maximize **Windows Explorer**.
   b) Navigate to **C:\091115Data\Connecting Drawings to External Data**.
   c) Double-click **Cinnamon Oil Project Milestones.mpp**.
      A timeline opens in Project.

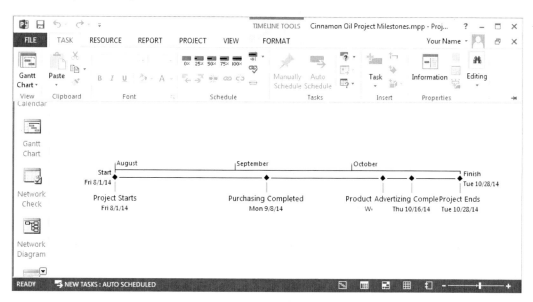

   d) Examine the timeline. Notice the milestones.
   e) Close Project.
   f) Minimize **Windows Explorer**.

2. Start a new drawing based on the **Timeline** template.
   a) Open Visio.
   b) On the Visio **Start** screen, in the **Search for online templates** field, type *timeline* and select the
      magnifying class icon.

c) Select the **Timeline** template.

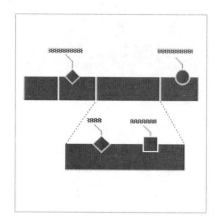

Timeline

d) In the **Timeline** preview, verify that the **US Units** radio button is selected.

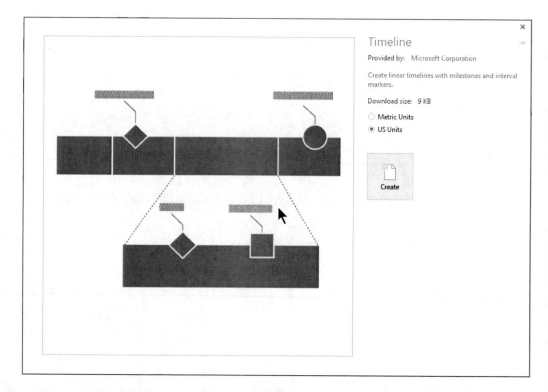

e) Select the **Create** button.
Visio opens a new drawing page and the **Timeline Shapes** stencil.

3. Use the **Import Timeline Wizard** to create a timeline.
   a) On the ribbon, select the **TIMELINE** tab.
   b) In the **Timeline** group, select the **Import Data** command.

c) In the **Import Timeline Wizard**, select the **Browse** button, navigate to **C:\091115Data\Connecting Drawings to External Data** and double-click **Cinnamon Oil Project Milestones.mpp**.

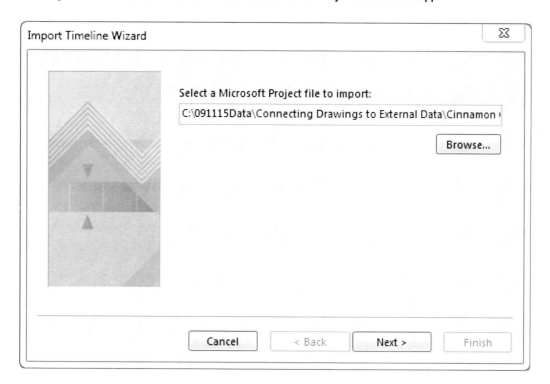

d) Select the **Next** button.
e) In the **Select task types to include** field, select **Milestones only**.

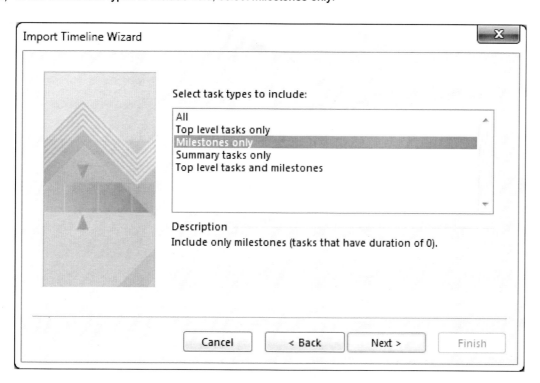

f) Select the **Next** button.

g) On the next screen, review the **Timeline**, **Milestone**, and **Interval** options, but don't make any changes.

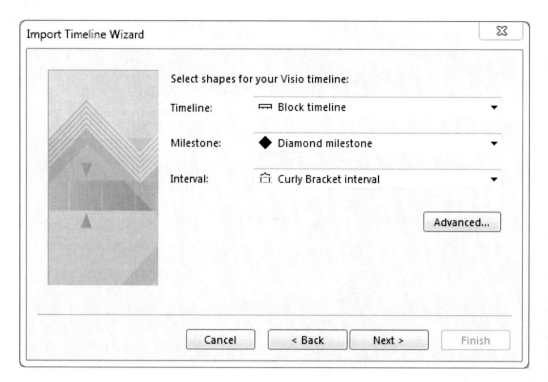

h) Select the **Next** button.

i) On the next screen, review the import properties.

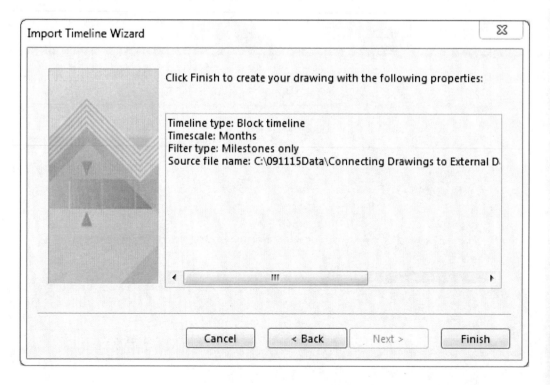

j) Select the **Finish** button.
Visio builds a timeline from the Project file.

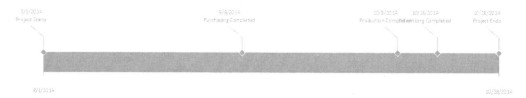

4. Increase the font size.
   a) Press the **Ctrl** and **A** keys to select all shapes in the drawing.
   b) On the ribbon, select the **HOME** tab.
   c) In the **Font** group, select the **Increase Font Size** icon A˙ several times until the font size is 12pt.

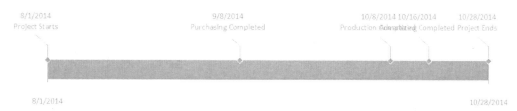

5. Move the text of the second and fourth milestones.
   a) Press the **Esc** key to deselect all shapes in the drawing.
   b) Select the second milestone's connector.
   c) Grab the **Reposition Text** handle at the top of connector.

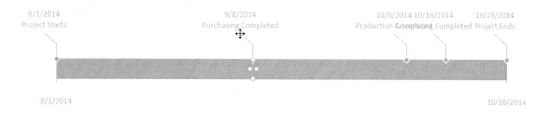

   d) Drag the text of the second below the timeline.

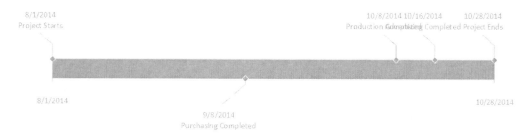

   e) Select the fourth milestone's connector.

f) Grab the **Reposition Text** handle at the top of connector.

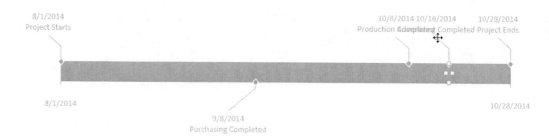

g) Drag the text of the fourth milestone below the timeline.

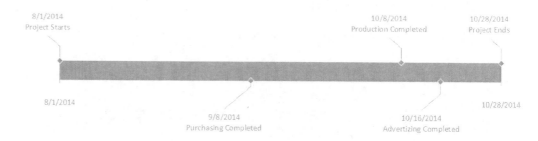

6. Save the file in the **C:\091115Data\Connecting Drawings to External Data** folder as *My Cinnamon Oil Project Timeline.vsdx*

7. Close Visio.

TOPIC E

Connect a Map to an Access Database

Displaying business information on maps can be a powerful tool; however, such maps are usually complex to build and difficult to update. By connecting a map to a Microsoft Access® database, you can automate its initial construction and subsequent maintenance.

Microsoft Access

Microsoft Access is powerful database creation and management program that is bundled with Microsoft Office Professional 2013. Information is stored in data tables that look much like spreadsheets, and the tables are connected through common fields.

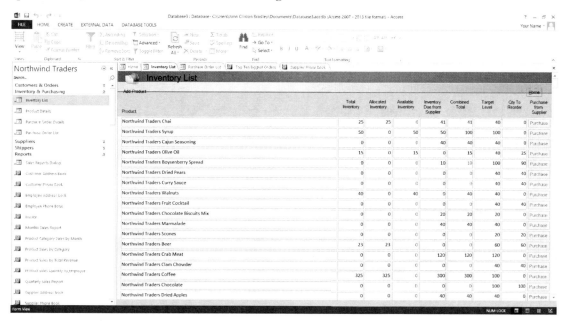

Figure 3-20: Microsoft Access 2013.

The DATA Tab

Visio's **DATA** tab consists of a number of commands for linking Access databases (and other data sources) to Visio drawings.

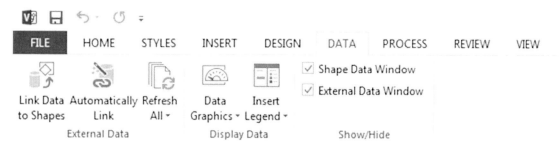

Figure 3-21: The DATA tab.

The following table briefly explains how you can use each command.

Command	Use
Link Data to Shapes	Run the **Data Selector** tool (which you learned about earlier in this lesson) to connect the drawing to an Access database (or other data source).
Automatically Link	Connect all shapes or selected shapes in the drawing with specified records in the data source.
Refresh All	Update a drawing to reflect changes made in the data source.
Data Graphics	Change how data is displayed in relation to shapes.
Insert Legend	Add a legend to the drawing that explains the data graphics.
Shape Data Window	Display or hide the **Shape Data Window**.
External Data Window	Display or hide the **External Data Window**.

The Automatically Link Data Tool

The **Automatically Link Data** tool enables you to connect shapes in the drawing with specific records in the data source. You can run this tool by selecting the **Automatically Link** tool on the **DATA** tab. The tool has three screens:

1. Choose to link selected shapes or all shapes on the page.
2. Map columns in the data source to fields in the shapes.
3. Finish.

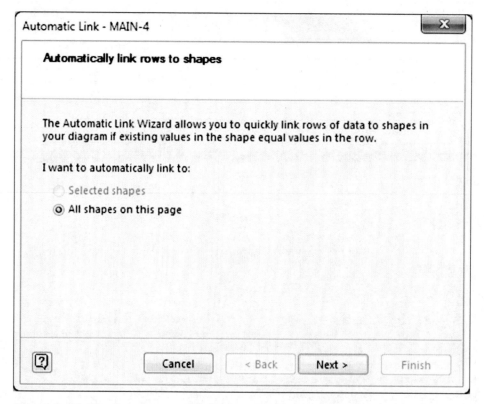

Figure 3–22: The first screen of the Automatically Link Data tool.

 Note: Before you can run this tool, you must first run the **Data Selector** tool by selecting the **Link Data to Shapes** command on the **DATA** tab.

Here's an example of how it works:

- You have a drawing that contains ten shapes representing the ten departments in an organization. Each shape has a data field labeled **DEPARTMENT**. The **DEPARTMENT** field in the each shape is populated by the name of the department—**Shipping & Receiving**, **Accounting**, **Marketing**, and so forth.
- You also have a table in an Access database linked to the drawing. The table consists of several fields, one of which is labeled **DEPARTMENT**. The table contains ten records with information about each department in your organization. The **DEPARTMENT** field in each record is populated by the name of the department—**Shipping & Receiving**, **Accounting**, **Marketing**, and so forth.
- The **Automatically Link Data** tool looks at the **DEPARTMENT** field in the Visio shapes and the **DEPARTMENT** field in the Access table. When the tool finds a matching value between the shape and a record, it creates a link.

 Note: Before running this tool, each shape must have at least one defined data field that maps to a column in the data source; and each shape must have a value in the defined data field that matches a record.

The Shape Data Window

The **Shape Data** window enables you to view and edit the data defined for a shape. If the **Shape Data Window** check box is checked on the **DATA** tab, the **Shape Data** window will appear whenever you select a shape. Be default, the window floats; but you can dock it on the top, left, or right of the screen if you wish. The left column in the window shows the data fields. The right column shows the value for each field. If you double-click a value, you can edit it.

Figure 3–23: The Shape Data window.

The External Data Window

After you run the **Data Selector** tool, Visio opens the **External Data** window at the bottom of the screen. You can also show and hide this window by checking or unchecking the **External Data Window** check box on the **DATA** tab. You can make the window taller or shorter if desired.

This window shows you the data source(s) linked to the drawing and the records in the data

source(s). If a record is linked to a shape, a link icon 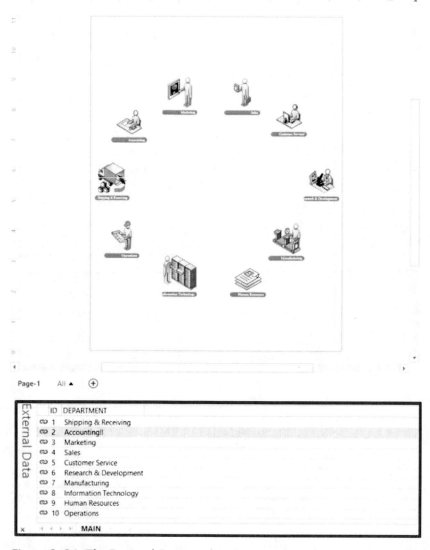 appears next to the record. If a record is not linked to a shape, you can link it by dragging its row from the **External Data** window and dropping it on the desired shape.

Figure 3–24: The External Data window.

Data Graphics

The **Data Graphics** command enables you to change how data is displayed in relation to shapes. When you select a shape (or shapes) and select the command, Visio displays a menu of options.

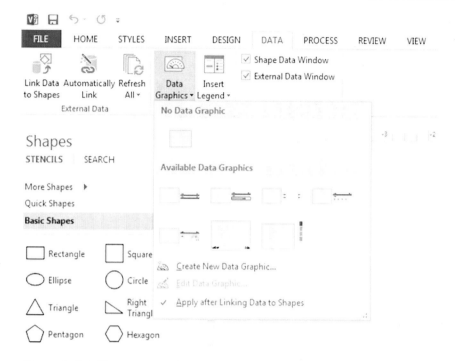

Figure 3-25: The Data Graphic menu.

This table explains the use of each option.

Option	Use
No Data Graphic	Turn off the display of data.
Available Data Graphics	Choose a data display format.
Create New Data Graphic	Build a new data display format. When you select this option, Visio opens a **New Data Graphic** dialog box. In this dialog box you can do the following (among others): • Choose which data fields to show. • Select a method for displaying each field. The options are **Text**, **Data Bar**, **Icon**, and **Color by Value**. • Pick a style of each method. • Fine-tune the style.
Edit Data Graphic	Change the data display format currently applied to the shape. When you select this option, Visio opens an **Edit Data Graphic** dialog box that is similar to the **New Data Graphic** dialog box.
Apply after Linking Data to Shapes	When this option is checked, Visio will apply the data graphic each time you link a record to a shape.

Legend Options

The **Insert Legend** command adds a legend to the drawing that explains the data graphics. When you select this command, Visio displays two options for the legend—**Horizontal** and **Vertical**. Depending on the data graphics, Visio may not allow you to add a legend or it may allow you to add only one of the options.

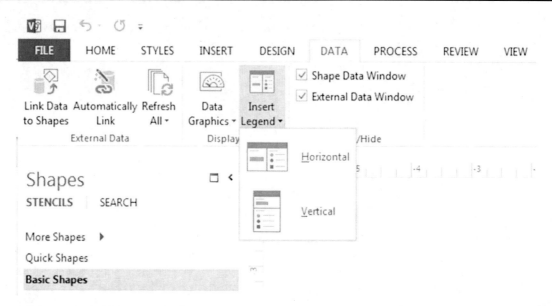

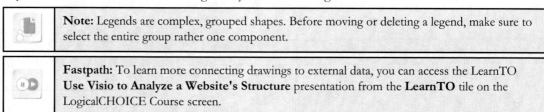

Figure 3-26: The Legend Options menu.

Visio always inserts a legend in the upper right corner of the drawing page. However, you can move it to another location if you wish. You can remove the legend by selecting it and pressing the **Delete** key. You can also edit the text in a legend by double-clicking it.

> **Note:** Legends are complex, grouped shapes. Before moving or deleting a legend, make sure to select the entire group rather one component.

> **Fastpath:** To learn more connecting drawings to external data, you can access the LearnTO **Use Visio to Analyze a Website's Structure** presentation from the **LearnTO** tile on the LogicalCHOICE Course screen.

> **Access the Checklist tile on your LogicalCHOICE course screen for reference information and job aids on How to Connect a Map to an Access Database.**

ACTIVITY 3-5
Connecting a Map to an Access Database

Data File

C:\091115Data\Connecting Drawings to External Data\EE Territories.accdb

Before You Begin

Visio is closed.

Scenario

Gary Thiele, the US and Canada sales manager, asks you to create a sales territory map of the United States that he can share with his sales representatives. There are ten territories, named Territory 0 through Territory 9. Because territory boundaries change frequently, Gary uses a Microsoft Access database to track which states are in each territory. This database resides on the company network.

Visio 2013 doesn't contain geographic map templates, stencils, or shapes. However, on the Microsoft website, you will find a Visio stencil for the United States.

Note: You can download free Visio map stencils at **http://www.microsoft.com/en-us/ download/details.aspx?id=13443**. **Maps_U.zip** contains United States and world maps in US units. **Maps_M.zip** contains United States and world maps in metric units.

---

1. Open the Access database.
   a) Maximize **Windows Explorer**.
   b) Navigate to **C:\091115Data\Connecting Drawings to External Data**.
   c) Double-click **EE Territories.accdb**.
      The database opens in Access.

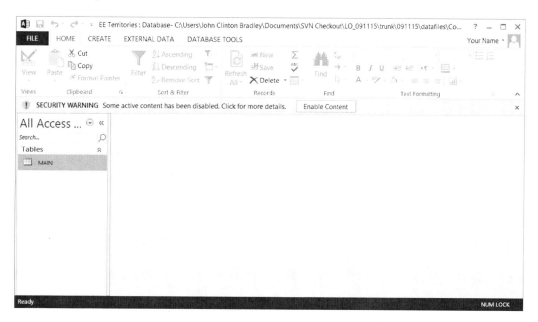

   d) If Access displays a security warning, select **Enable Content**.

e) In the **Tables** pane, double-click **MAIN**.
The MAIN table opens.

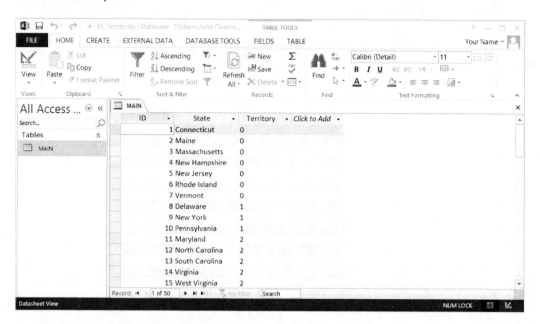

f) Examine the table. Notice the column names.
g) Minimize Access.
h) Close **Windows Explorer**.

2. Open Visio and start a new, blank drawing.

3. Change the page orientation from portrait to landscape.
a) On the ribbon, select the **DESIGN** tab.
b) In the **Page Setup** group, select **Orientation→Landscape**.

4. Download the US Map stencil.
a) Open **Internet Explorer**.
b) Navigate to http://www.bing.com.
c) Use Bing to search for *visio map stencils*
d) Select the **Download Geographic Map Shapes for Microsoft Visio from** search result.

Download Geographic **Map** Shapes for Microsoft **Visio** from ...
www.microsoft.com/en-us/download/details.aspx?id=13443 ▼
Download Geographic **Map** Shapes for Microsoft **Visio** from Official Microsoft Download
Center ... The **stencils** will be listed in the My Shapes menu.
4.1 MB · Version 1.0 · Published Oct 26, 2009 · System Requirements

e) Verify that you are in the **Microsoft Download Center** and are on the **Geographic Map Shapes for Microsoft Visio** page.

The URL is **http://www.microsoft.com/en-us/download/details.aspx?id=13443**.

f) In the **Select Language** field, verify that **English** is selected.

g) Select **Download**.

h) On the **Choose the download you want** page, check the **Maps_U.zip** check box.

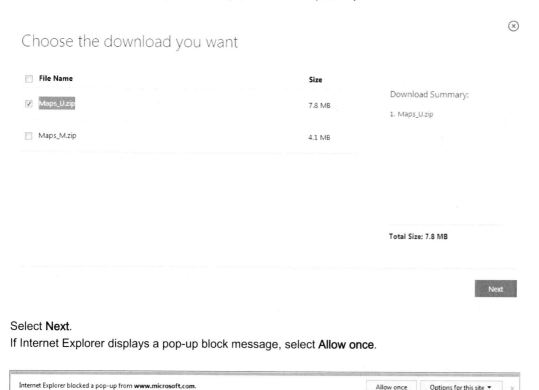

i) Select **Next**.

j) If Internet Explorer displays a pop-up block message, select **Allow once**.

k) When Internet Explorer asks whether you want to open or save the file, select **Save**.

Do you want to open or save **Maps_U.zip** (7.81 MB) from **download.microsoft.com**? | Open | Save ▼ | Cancel | ×

l) When Internet Explorer says the download is complete, select **Open**.

The Maps_U (2).zip download has completed. | Open ▼ | Open folder | View downloads | ×

m) If Windows displays a **How do you want to open this type of file (.zip)?** message, select **File Explorer**.

The zip file opens in **Windows Explorer**, showing two Visio stencil files.

n) In the left pane of **Windows Explorer**, expand **This PC→Documents**.

Note: Select the right arrow icon to expand both the **This PC** and **Documents** folders. If you select the **This PC** or **Documents** folder directly, Windows will display the contents of the selected folder in the right pane—so you will no longer see the two Visio stencil files. Should this happen, select the **Back** button one or more times until you can again see the two Visio templates in **Downloads\Maps_U.zip**.

o) Drag **United States Maps (US units).vss** to the **My Shapes** folder.

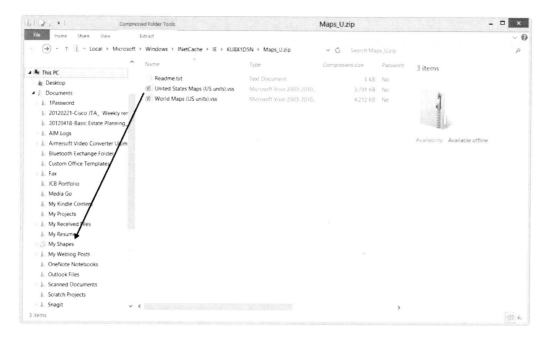

5. Open the US Map stencil.

   a) In the **Shapes** window, select **More Shapes→Open Stencil**.

b) In the **Open Stencil** dialog box, navigate to **C:\091115Data\Connecting Drawings to External Data** and double-click **United States Maps (US units).vss**.
The **United States Maps** stencil opens in the **Shapes** window.

6. Add the United States shape to the drawing page.

a) In the **Shapes** window, select the **United States** master shape and drag it to the top left corner of the drawing page.

b) Resize the United States shape so that its width is about the same as the width of the drawing page.

7. Ungroup the United States shape.

   a) Verify that the United States shape is selected.

   b) Right-click the shape and, from the shortcut menu, select **Group→Ungroup**. Visio displays a warning dialog box.

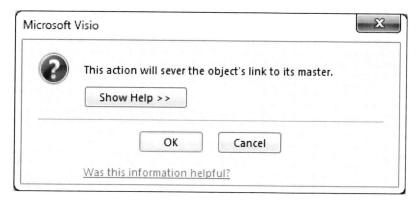

c) Select **OK**.
    Visio breaks the group into individual shapes.

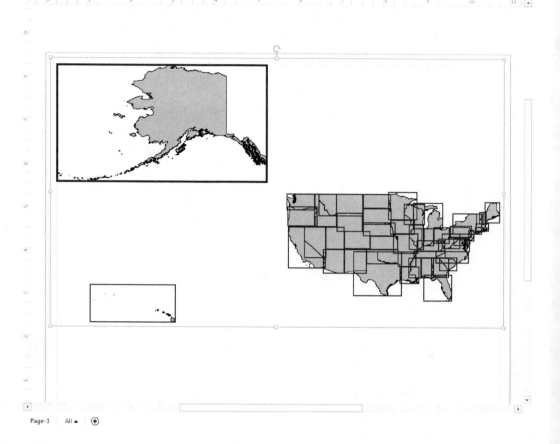

d) Press the **Esc** key to deselect all of the shapes.

8. Open the **Shape Data Window**.

    a) On the ribbon, select the **DATA** tab.

b) In the **Show/Hide** group, check the **Shape Data Window** check box.

Notice that a floating **SHAPE DATA** window opens. Because no shape is selected, the window says there isn't any shape data.

9. Examine shape data properties.
   a) Select the Alaska shape.
   In the **SHAPE DATA** window, notice that the only data element is the **Name** field, which has the value of **Alaska**.

   b) Select two or three other state shapes of your choice.
   In the **SHAPE DATA** window, notice that each shape has a single data element, the **Name** field, which is populated by the state's name.
   c) Close the **SHAPE DATA** window.

10. Use the **Data Selector** tool to connect state shapes to the Access database.
   a) Select all 50 state shapes on the drawing page by pressing the **Ctrl** and **A** keys.
   b) On the **DATA** tab, in the **External Data** group, select the **Link Data to Shapes** command.
   Visio opens the **Data Selector** dialog box.

c) On the **What data do you want to use?** screen, select the **Microsoft Access database** radio button.

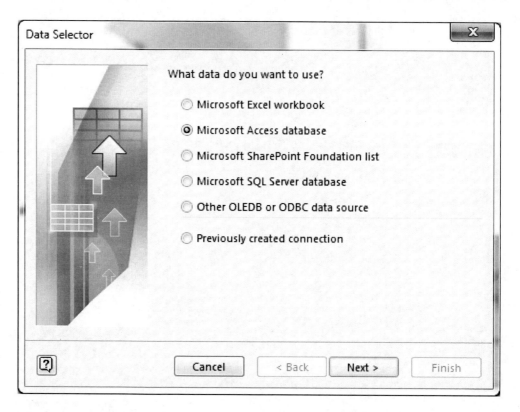

d) Select the **Next** button.
e) Below the **What database do you want to use?** field, select the **Browse** button, navigate to **C:\091115Data\Connecting Drawings to External Data** and double-click **EE Territories.accdb**.

f) Review the **What table to you want to import?** field.

The database contains only the MAIN table, so the correct table is selected.

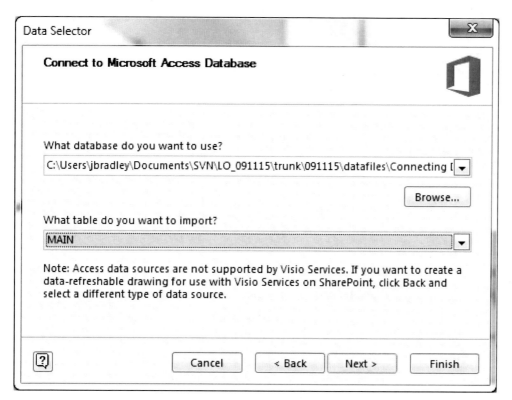

g) Select the **Next** button.

h) Review the next screen of the **Data Selector**.

You want to use all columns and rows in the **MAIN** table, so no changes are needed.

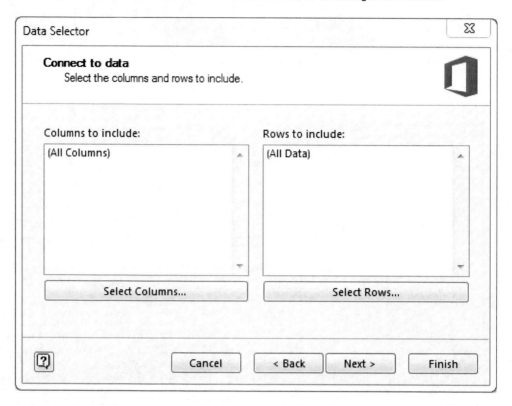

i) Select the **Next** button.

The **Data Selector** says that you successfully imported your data.

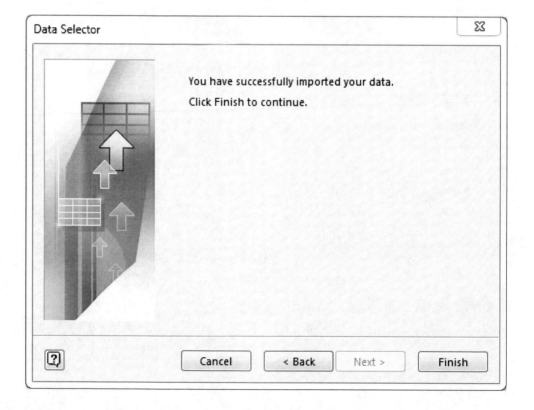

j) Select the **Finish** button.
    Visio opens the **External Data Window** below the drawing page.

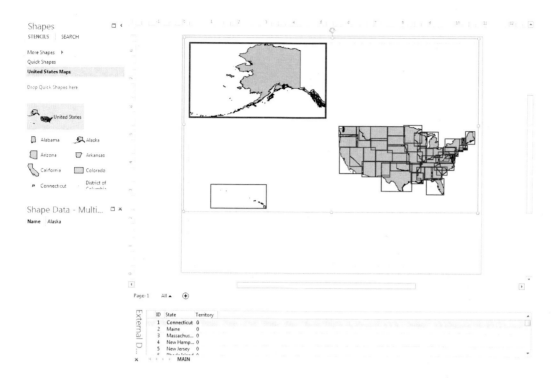

11. Use the **Automatically Link** tool to link each state shape to a record in the database table.

    a) On the **DATA** tab, in the **External Data** group, select the **Automatically Link** command.

b) In the **Automatic Link** dialog box, review the options.

Since all 50 state shapes on the page are already selected, it doesn't matter which radio button is selected.

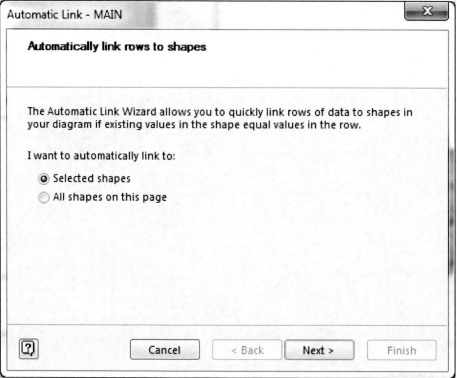

c) Select the **Next** button.
d) On the next screen, under **Data Column**, select the drop-down field and select the **State** option.

e) Under **Shape Field**, select the drop-down field and select the **Name** option.

Since the shapes aren't currently linked, it doesn't matter whether the **Replace existing links** check box is checked or unchecked.

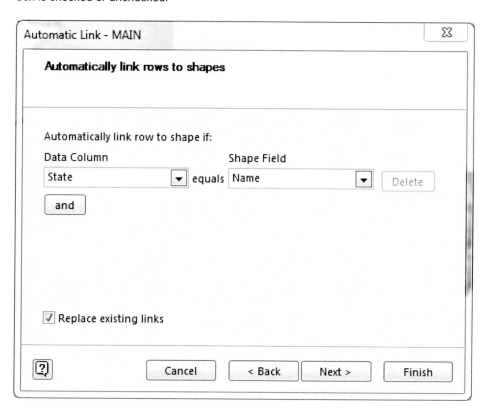

f) Select the **Next** button.

g) On the next screen, review the options you selected.
   No changes are needed.

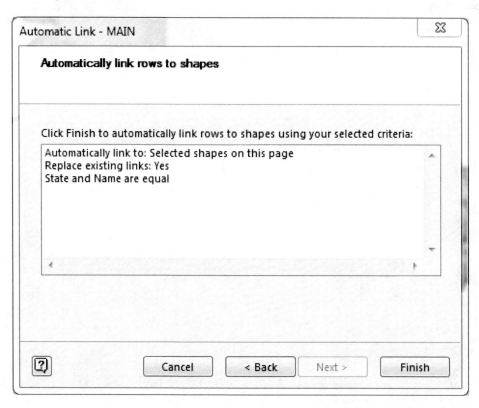

h) Select the **Finish** button.

In the **External Data Window**, notice that Visio has linked every state shape with a row in the Access table. Visio also displays the linked data for each shape as text.

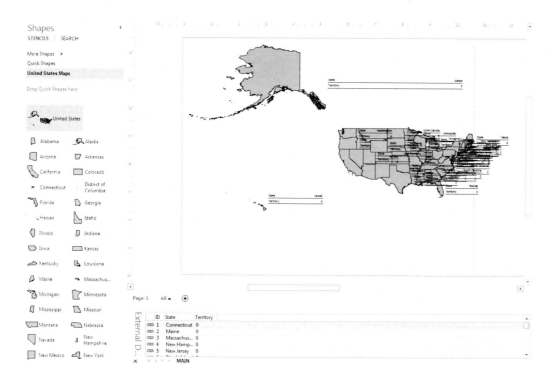

> **Note:** You may close the **External Data Window** at this point if desired. To do this, on the ribbon, select the **DATA** tab and in the **Show/Hide** group, uncheck the **External Data Window** check box.

12. Change the data graphics.

   a) In the **Display Data** group, select **Data Graphics→Create New Data Graphic**.

b) In the **New Data Graphic** dialog box, select **New Item**.

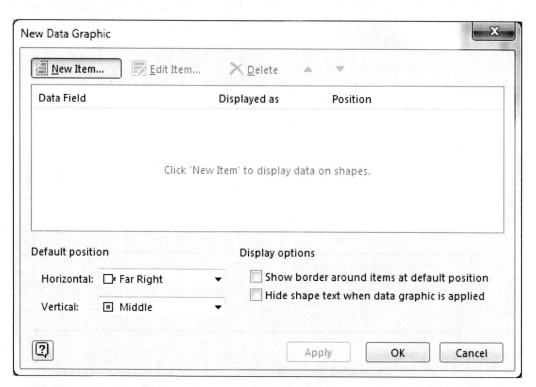

c) In the **New Item** dialog box, select the **Data field** drop-down field and select the **Territory** option.
d) Select the **Displayed as** drop-down field and select the **Color by Value** option. Visio displays the **Color assignments** section.

Visio displays the **Coloring method** field.

e) In the **Coloring method** field, select the **Each color represents a unique value** option.
   Visio displays assigns a different color to each territory.

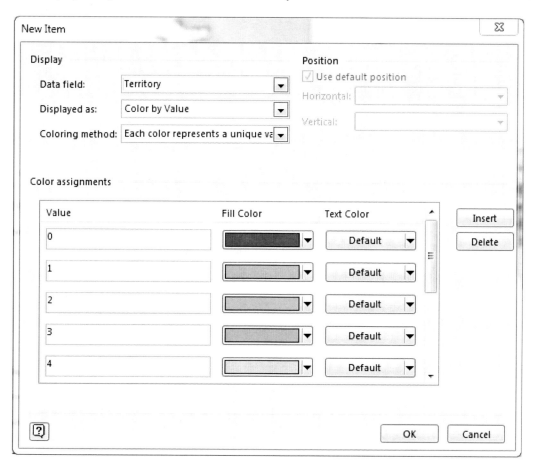

f) Select **OK** to close the **New Item** dialog box.
    Visio displays the new item in **New Data Graphic** dialog box.

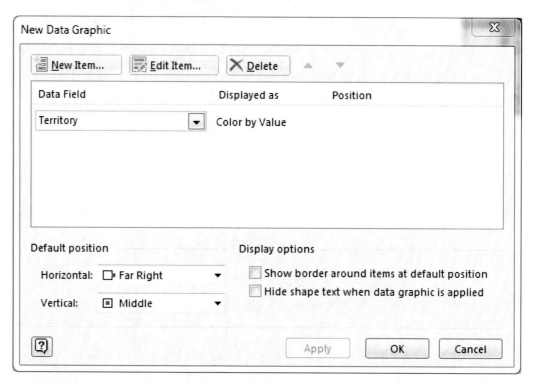

g) Select **OK**.
    Visio displays a dialog box asking if you want to apply the new data graphic to the selected shapes.

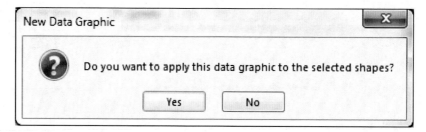

h) Select **Yes**.
    Visio applies a color to each state shape based on the territory value in the database table.

i) Press the **Esc** key to deselect the shapes in the drawing.

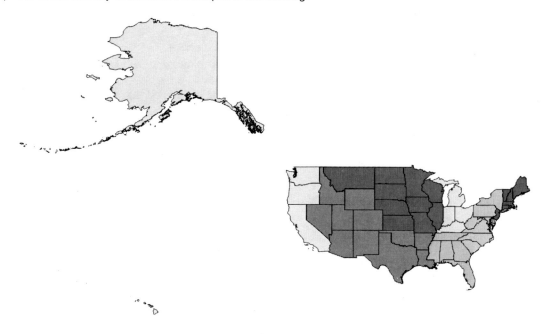

13. Add a legend to the map.

a) On the **DATA** tab, in the **Display Data** group, select **Insert Legend→Vertical**.
Visio inserts the legend in the upper right corner of the drawing page, obscuring the map.

b) Move the legend to the lower left corner of the drawing page.

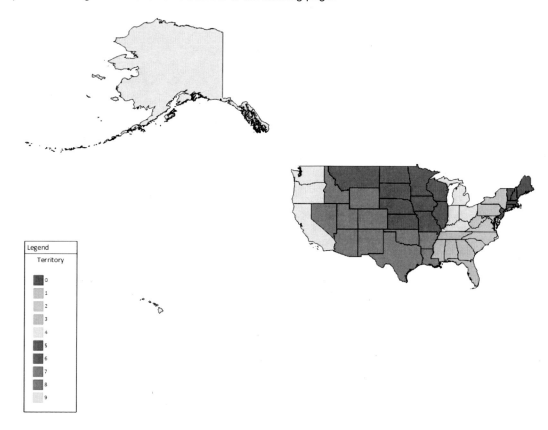

14. Make a change to the Access database and see the change on the Visio map.

a) In the Visio map, notice that Nevada is colored orange because it's in Territory 8. Gary Thiele wants to reassign Nevada to Territory 9.
b) Maximize Access.
c) In the **MAIN** table, scroll down to Nevada. It should be record 42 of 50.
d) In the **Nevada** row, in the **Territory** column, double-click the cell.
e) Change the value from 8 to 9.
Access displays a pencil icon to indicate that the record is being edited.

	ID ▾	State ▾	Territory ▾
	36	Louisiana	7
	37	Oklahoma	7
	38	Texas	7
	39	Arizona	8
	40	Colorado	8
	41	Idaho	8
	42	Nevada	9
	43	New Mexico	8
	44	Utah	8
	45	Wyoming	8
	46	Alaska	9
	47	California	9
	48	Hawaii	9
	49	Oregon	9
	50	Washington	9

f) Press **Enter** to complete the edit.
The pencil icon disappears and the focus moves to record 43.

g) In the **Quick Access Toolbar**, select the **Save** icon 💾.
h) Close Access.

i) In Visio, on the ribbon, select the **DATA** tab if necessary.
j) In the **External Data** group, select the **Refresh All** command.

Refresh
All ▾

k) If Visio displays a security notice, read it and select **OK**.

l) In the **Refresh Data** dialog box, select **Refresh All** and then **Close**.

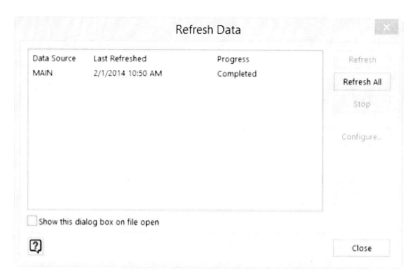

Notice that Nevada is now colored yellow, indicating that is in Territory 9.

15. Save the drawing in the **C:\091115Data\Connecting Drawings to External Data** folder as *My EE Territories Map.vsdx*

16. Close the drawing.

Summary

In this lesson, you learned how to make drawings automatically from external data. These skills are especially useful when you need to repeatedly update your drawings. Automating drawings in Visio can potentially save you a lot of work.

What types of data sources are used in your company?

What kinds of drawings might you link to your company's data sources?

 Note: Check your LogicalCHOICE Course screen for opportunities to interact with your classmates, peers, and the larger LogicalCHOICE online community about the topics covered in this course or other topics you are interested in. From the Course screen you can also access available resources for a more continuous learning experience.

4 | Leveraging Development Tools

Lesson Time: 1 hour, 45 minutes

Lesson Objectives

In this lesson, you will leverage development tools. You will:

- Create macros.

- Modify ShapeSheets.

- Build advanced shapes.

Lesson Introduction

Like all products in the Microsoft Office suite, Visio is an extremely robust program. Many users never take full advantage of Visio's capabilities. Even if you aren't a programmer, it is good to become aware of Visio's advanced capabilities so that you can use them when need them.

TOPIC A

Create Macros

As you work with Visio more, you may find that much of your effort involves repetitive, time-consuming tasks. Macros can save you time by automating such repetitive tasks.

The DEVELOPER Tab

Visio's **DEVELOPER** tab enables you to perform a number of advanced functions, such as creating macros, modifying ShapeSheets, and building advanced shapes. By default, this tab is hidden on the ribbon. You must go to the **Backstage** (**FILE→Options→Customize Ribbon**) and unhide this tab before you can use it.

Figure 4-1: The DEVELOPER tab.

Macros

You may be familiar with macros from other Microsoft® Office applications. A *macro* is a series of commands that you can record to automate a repetitive task, and then run when you need to perform the task. Here are just a few examples how you might use macros in Visio:

- Duplicate a page.
- Add a custom shape with a set size and color to a drawing page.
- Set the zoom factor of all pages to 100 percent.
- Paste text as unformatted.

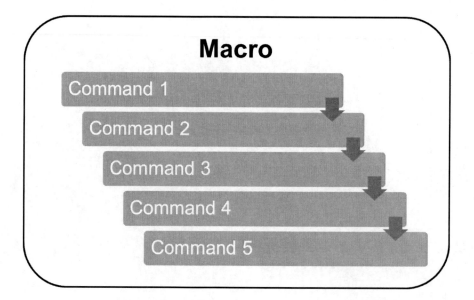

Figure 4-2: An illustration of a macro as a series of commands.

Macro Commands

The **Record Macro** command enables you to start creating a macro. When you select this command, a **Record Macro** dialog box opens.

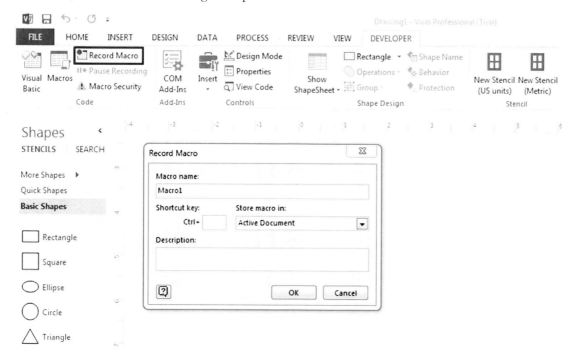

Figure 4-3: The Record Macro command and dialog box.

This table explains each field of the dialog box.

Field	Explanation
Macro name	Visio will suggest a name (such as Macro1) but you can type over the suggested name with one that it more meaningful (such as PageDuplicator). Macro names can't contain spaces or special characters.
Shortcut key	If you wish, you can assign a keyboard shortcut to the new macro (such as **Ctrl+m**). This enables you to quickly activate the macro without having to run it from the **Macros** command on the **DEVELOPER** tab.
Store macro in	You can save the new macro in an open drawing, stencil, or template. By default, Visio will save the macro in the active drawing.
Description	It's a good idea to describe what the macro does, in case you forget or another Visio user encounters the macro in your document.

After you complete the **Record Macro** dialog box, you'll need to perform the actions you want captured. If necessary, you can temporarily suspend capture by selecting **Pause Recording**. When you're ready to continue capture, select **Resume Recorder**. To complete the macro, select **Stop Recording**.

You can run the macro in two ways:

- By using the keyboard shortcut you assigned while you were creating the macro.
- By using the **Macros** command and dialog box on the **DEVELOPER** tab.

Visual Basic for Applications

Visio records macros in the Visual Basic for Applications (VBA) programming language. If the macro fails for some reason, Visio will open the **Microsoft Visual Basic for Applications** program so that you can debug the macro. As you become more familiar with the VBA language, you will find the information and tools provided by the debugging environment helpful and informative.

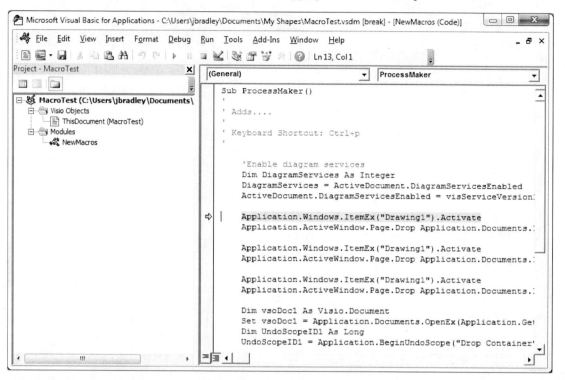

Figure 4-4: A macro being debugged in the VBA program.

Macros Security

As with most programming code, hackers have found ways to use VBA code for unethical and illegal purposes. If an unsuspecting user opens a Visio drawing containing a malicious macro, intellectual property may be lost or a virus could be introduced. To mitigate this risk, macros are automatically disabled by default in Visio. If you open a Visio file that contains a macro, Visio will display a security notice. You can choose to enable the content if you wish, but you shouldn't unless you're sure the drawing is from a trusted source and the macro it contains is benign.

You can change your macro security settings by selecting the **Macro Security** command on **DEVELOPER** tab. This opens on the **Macro Setting** tab of the **Trust Center** dialog box.

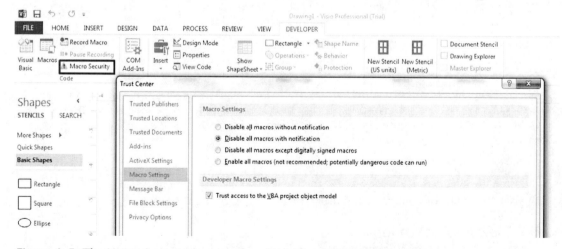

Figure 4-5: The Macro Security command and the Trust Center dialog box.

The following table describes the available options.

Option	Description
Disable all macros without notification	Visio disables the macros in a drawing without giving you the option to enable them.
Disable all macros with notification	This is the default. Visio disables the macros in a drawing but gives you the option to enable them.
Disable all macros except digitally signed macros	Visio disables all macros in a drawing except those digitally signed by a trusted source.
Enable all macros	Visio enables all macros in a drawing. This setting is NOT recommended.
Trust access to the VBA project object model	VBA enables macros with Visio documents to perform operations in a Visio document, but Visio (and other applications that can be automated through VBA) can also be controlled from outside of Visio—by a different application. The **Trust access to the VBA project object model** option provides a further level of protection that essentially blocks access to all VBA objects by any automation client. A user could disable (uncheck) this option to prevent external programs from using Visio's VBA model to cause harm. Of course, doing so will prevent automation through VBA.

Macros and Visio File Formats

As an additional layer of security, Visio makes a clear distinction between file formats that are macro-free and macro-enabled. This table shows the six formats grouped by their macro capabilities.

Macro-Free File Formats	Macro-Enabled File Formats
• Visio Drawing (*.vsdx) • Visio Stencil (*.vssx) • Visio Template (*.vstx)	• Visio Macro-Enabled Drawing (*.vsdm) • Visio Macro-Enabled Stencil (*.vssm) • Visio Macro-Enabled Template (*.vstm)

If you recorded a macro that you want to save for later use, you must save it the appropriate macro-enabled file form. If you attempt to save a file that contains a macro in a standard (macro-free) format, Visio will display a warning message. If you choose to save the file in a standard format, the macro will be lost.

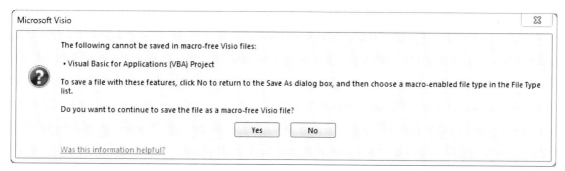

Figure 4–6: The file format warning message.

> Access the **Checklist** tile on your **LogicalCHOICE** course screen for reference information and job aids on How to Create Macros.

ACTIVITY 4-1
Creating Macros

Data File

C:\091115Data\Leveraging Development Tools\Macros.vsdm

Before You Begin

Visio Professional 2013 is open.

Scenario

As your company's warehouse operations grow, your team has its hands full documenting storage locations. Each storage bin has a different number of compartments, arranged in columns and rows. Each time you create a new bin diagram, you have to create a grid, as shown.

Bin Contents: Bottleneck Labels Bin Location: Warehouse 13, Rack E32, Level 2						
A1 Gold labels for Size A6 bottles	B1 Gold labels for Size A7 bottles	C1 Emerald labels for Size A7 bottles	D1 Standard seal for all bottles	E1 1/8" emerald ribbon	F1 1/8" emerald ribbon	G1 Emerald Crown wrapper
A2 Gold labels for Size A6 bottles	B2 Gold labels for Size A7 bottles	C2 Emerald labels for Size A7 bottles	D2 Standard seal for all bottles	E2 1/8" emerald ribbon	F2 1/8" emerald ribbon	G2 Emerald Crown wrapper
A3 Gold labels for Size A6 bottles	B3 Gold labels for Size A7 bottles	C3 Emerald labels for Size A7 bottles	D3 Standard seal for all bottles	E3 1/8" emerald ribbon	F3 1/8" emerald ribbon	G3 Emerald Crown wrapper
A4 Silver labels for Size A6 bottles	B4 Silver labels for Size A7 bottles	C4 Emerald labels for Size A7 bottles	D4 Standard seal for all bottles	E4 1/8" emerald ribbon	F4 1/8" emerald ribbon	G4 Emerald Crown wrapper
A5 Silver labels for Size A6 bottles	B5 Silver labels for Size A7 bottles	C5 Emerald labels for Size A7 bottles	D5 Standard seal for all bottles	E5 1/8" emerald ribbon	F5 1/8" emerald ribbon	G5 Emerald Crown wrapper

Some bins have only one compartment. Others may have up to 12 rows and 12 columns of compartments. A macro would save you some time by automating the steps to create these grids.

You have decided to create a macro that will:

- Ask the user for the number of columns and rows in the bin, as well as a description of the general bin contents and location.
- Determine how wide and tall the current Visio page is.
- Draw a box on the page for each compartment.
- Arrange and size each compartment to fill the available page width and height.
- Label each compartment by column (a letter) and row (a number).

Although macro development often requires that you write programming code, you can often get a good start on a macro by turning on the macro recorder and performing the steps as Visio writes code for you.

1. Prepare to record a macro.

   a) Create a new Visio document based on the **Blank Drawing** template.

   To record a macro, you must have a document in which you will model the steps to be recorded. You also need to enable the DEVELOPER tab, which contains commands you will use to record and edit macros.

   b) On the ribbon, select **FILE**.

   c) In the **Backstage** view, select **Options**.

   The Visio Options dialog box is shown.

   d) In the **Visio Options** dialog box, select **Customize Ribbon**.

   e) In the right pane, check the **Developer** option.

   f) Select **OK**.

   The **DEVELOPER** tab has been added to the ribbon.

   g) On the ribbon, select the **DEVELOPER** tab.

   This tab includes various advanced options that are provided for programming and automating Visio. It is hidden by default in a new Visio installation.

2. Start recording the macro.

   a) On the **DEVELOPER** tab, in the **Code** group, select the **Record Macro** command.

   You are prompted to provide information in the **Record Macro** dialog box.

   b) Replace the text in the **Macro name** text box with *StorageDiagram*

   Your macro name should describe what the macro does. If you need to clarify the name, you can change it later.

   c) In the **Shortcut key** text box, type *V*

   Make sure you type an *uppercase* V. The resulting shortcut will be shown as **Ctrl+Shift+V**. **Ctrl** is always added automatically, so do not press **Ctrl** when you enter this value.

   d) Notice where the macro will be stored.

By default, the macro is stored in the active document—the document you are currently editing. If other documents are open or stencils are attached, they will appear in the **Store macro in** drop-down list.

e) In the **Description** text box, type *Make storage diagram*

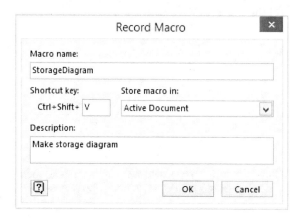

f) Select **OK**.

The **Record Macro** button has been replaced with a **Stop Recording** button, which indicates that the macro is now being recorded. The macro does not record timing, so you do not need to rush when recording the macro. When the macro runs, it will run as quickly as the computer allows, without adding timing delays you introduced when you recorded it.

3. Perform steps that should be included in the macro.

a) On the **DEVELOPER** tab, in the **Shape Design** group, select the **Rectangle** tool.

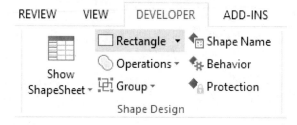

b) In the upper-left corner of the drawing, draw a rectangle that is about 1-1/2 inches wide and 1 inch tall.

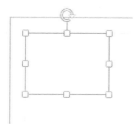

The size does not have to be perfect. You can edit the macro code later to specify an exact size.

c) Right-click the new shape and select **Edit Text**.

d) Type *A1*

e) Press **Esc** to stop editing the text.

f) On the ribbon, in the **Code** group, select **Stop Recording**.

4. Clear the drawing area and save the document in preparation for testing the macro.

a) On the ribbon, select the **HOME** tab.

b) In the **Tools** group, select the **Pointer** tool.

c) Delete the process box you created while you were recording the macro.

The steps that created the process box have been recorded in the macro. You will try to create a new copy of the process box by using your recorded macro.

5. Save as a macro-enabled document.

a) On the ribbon, select **FILE** and then select **Save As**.

b) Select **Browse** and browse to **C:\091115Data\Leveraging Development Tools**.

c) In the **Save as type** drop-down list, select **Visio Macro-Enabled Drawing (*.vsdm)**.

To enable your macros to run, the document must be saved in the macro-enabled format.

d) Change the text in the **File name** text box to *My Macro Diagram*

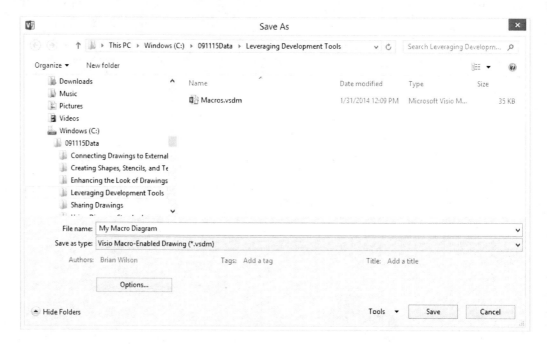

e) Select **Save**.

6. Attempt to run the recorded macro.

a) Press **Ctrl+Shift+V** to run the macro.

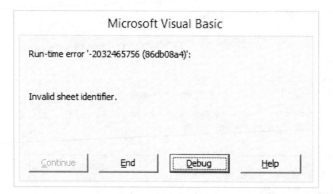

The macro starts to run, but an error is encountered. It is fairly common in Visio for a recorded macro to fail. You often need to make some minor programming adjustments to get a recorded macro to work correctly.

7. Debug the recorded macro.

a) Select **Debug** to show the VBA programming editor.

```
Sub StorageDiagram()
'
' Make storage diagram
'
' Keyboard Shortcut: Ctrl+Shift+V
'

    'Enable diagram services
    Dim DiagramServices As Integer
    DiagramServices = ActiveDocument.DiagramServicesEnabled
    ActiveDocument.DiagramServicesEnabled = visServiceVersion140 + visServiceVersion150

    Application.ActiveWindow.Page.DrawRectangle 0.25, 10.75, 1.65625, 9.75

    Dim vsoCharacters1 As Visio.Characters
    Set vsoCharacters1 = Application.ActiveWindow.Page.Shapes.ItemFromID(1).Characters
    vsoCharacters1.Begin = 0
    vsoCharacters1.End = 0
    vsoCharacters1.Text = "A1"

    Application.ActiveWindow.DeselectAll

    'Restore diagram services
    ActiveDocument.DiagramServicesEnabled = DiagramServices

End Sub
```

The step that failed is highlighted.

Because you know the steps you recorded, even without knowing how to program VBA code, you can get a sense of what some of the individual steps do. For example, it is fairly evident that the `Application.ActiveWindow.Page.DrawRectangle` statement draws a rectangle. The numbers after that statement identify the boundaries of the rectangle. Your numbers may be slightly different from those shown here because the macro recorder noted the dimensions you used when manually drawing the rectangle.

It appears that the macro failed before the "A1" text was entered into the rectangle, because the highlighted command appears before the command that enters the text (`vsoCharacters1.Text = "A1"`).

The step that failed (shown with an arrow and highlighted) refers to a specific shape (`Shapes.ItemFromID(1)`). While the shape had this ID when the macro was recorded, it does not have this ID now that you are playing the macro. You can fix this with just a few edits to the code.

Do not be concerned if the reason for the macro failing is not clear at this time. It takes some knowledge of VBA to debug a recorded macro.

b) Select **Run→Reset** to stop the macro.

You are returned to the Visio drawing area. The macro failed partway through, leaving a rectangle on the page.

c) Press **Esc** to leave text editing mode. Select and delete the box so the drawing area is empty again.

8. Revise the recorded macro code.

a) On the ribbon, select the **DEVELOPER** tab. In the **Code** group, select **Visual Basic**.

The VBA programming editor is shown again.

b) Revise the highlighted statement as shown.

```
Sub StorageDiagram()
'
' Make storage diagram
'
' Keyboard Shortcut: Ctrl+Shift+V
'

    'Enable diagram services
    Dim DiagramServices As Integer
    DiagramServices = ActiveDocument.DiagramServicesEnabled
    ActiveDocument.DiagramServicesEnabled = visServiceVersion140 + visServiceVersion150

    Set myNewRect = Application.ActiveWindow.Page.DrawRectangle(0.25, 10.75, 1.65625, 9.75)

    Dim vsoCharacters1 As Visio.Characters
    Set vsoCharacters1 = Application.ActiveWindow.Page.Shapes.ItemFromID(1).Characters
    vsoCharacters1.Begin = 0
    vsoCharacters1.End = 0
    vsoCharacters1.Text = "A1"

    Application.ActiveWindow.DeselectAll

    'Restore diagram services
    ActiveDocument.DiagramServicesEnabled = DiagramServices

End Sub
```

Three sections of code you need to add to this statement are shown underlined.

Do not be concerned if the numbers provided to your DrawRectangle function are not exactly the same as the numbers shown here.

Instead of just drawing the new rectangle, the modified statement will now "remember" the new rectangle within a container named myNewRect. Now, instead of referring to the shape by its ID (which clearly is not working), you will modify the macro to refer to the shape by using the name myNewRect.

c) Select the code exactly as shown.

```
Sub StorageDiagram()
'
' Make storage diagram
'
' Keyboard Shortcut: Ctrl+Shift+V
'

    'Enable diagram services
    Dim DiagramServices As Integer
    DiagramServices = ActiveDocument.DiagramServicesEnabled
    ActiveDocument.DiagramServicesEnabled = visServiceVersion140 + visServiceVersion150

    Set myNewRect = Application.ActiveWindow.Page.DrawRectangle(0.25, 10.75, 1.65625, 9.75)

    Dim vsoCharacters1 As Visio.Characters
    Set vsoCharacters1 = Application.ActiveWindow.Page.Shapes.ItemFromID(1).Characters
    vsoCharacters1.Begin = 0
    vsoCharacters1.End = 0
    vsoCharacters1.Text = "A1"

    Application.ActiveWindow.DeselectAll

    'Restore diagram services
    ActiveDocument.DiagramServicesEnabled = DiagramServices

End Sub
```

The selected code is supposed to refer to the new shape, but it does not work as recorded. You will replace it with the myNewRect, which identifies the new rectangle.

d) Replace the selected code with *myNewRect*, as shown.

```
Sub StorageDiagram()
'
' Make storage diagram
'
' Keyboard Shortcut: Ctrl+Shift+V
'

    'Enable diagram services
    Dim DiagramServices As Integer
    DiagramServices = ActiveDocument.DiagramServicesEnabled
    ActiveDocument.DiagramServicesEnabled = visServiceVersion140 + visServiceVersion150

    Set myNewRect = Application.ActiveWindow.Page.DrawRectangle(0.25, 10.75, 1.65625, 9.75)

    Dim vsoCharacters1 As Visio.Characters
    Set vsoCharacters1 = myNewRect.Characters
    vsoCharacters1.Begin = 0
    vsoCharacters1.End = 0
    vsoCharacters1.Text = "A1"

    Application.ActiveWindow.DeselectAll

    'Restore diagram services
    ActiveDocument.DiagramServicesEnabled = DiagramServices

End Sub
```

e) In the **Microsoft Visual Basic for Applications** window, select **File→Save C:\091115Data\Leveraging Development Tools\My Macro Diagram.vsdm**.

f) In the **Microsoft Visual Basic for Applications** window, select **File→Close and Return to Visio**.

9. Test the revised macro.

a) In the **DEVELOPER** tab, in the **Code** group, select **Macros**.

Macros   ☒

Macro name:

My_Macro_Diagram.NewMacros.StorageDiagram

My_Macro_Diagram.NewMacros.Storage

Step Into

Edit

Create

Delete

Options...

Macros in: Active Document ⌄

Description
Make storage diagram

⁇   Run   Cancel

You used the keyboard shortcut to run the macro before, but this is another way to run a macro. It is useful when a macro does not have a keyboard shortcut assigned to it. It is also useful when you do not know what macros a document contains.

Your macro is the only one in this document, and it is selected already. You can see the description you wrote in the Description text area.

b) Select **Run**.

The macro runs and creates a text box.

c) Run the macro again.

It appears that nothing has happened because the macro ran so fast.

d) Drag the A1 box to the right.

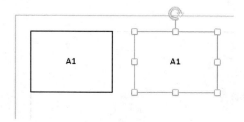

The previous box is revealed.

Your macro is well on its way to producing a grid. To develop this further, you would write some VBA code to prompt the user to provide the number of columns and rows. Then you would write code to create, position, and label the boxes as needed.

e) Save and close **My Macro Diagram.vsdm**.

10. Try out the completed macro.

a) From the **C:\091115Data\Leveraging Development Tools** directory, open **Macros.vsdm**.

b) This document contains a finished version of the macro. One bin diagram page has already been created.

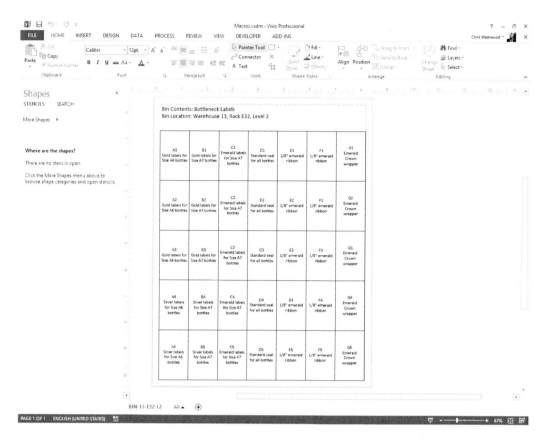

c) On the ribbon, from the **INSERT** tab, in the **Pages** group, select **New Page**.

You will create a new bin diagram on this page.

d) On the ribbon, from the **DEVELOPER** tab, in the **Code** group, select **Macros**.

The finished macro, which has been named **EE.AddDiagram.BinStorage**, is selected.

e) Select **Run**.

You are prompted to enter the number of columns in the bin.

f) Type *4*

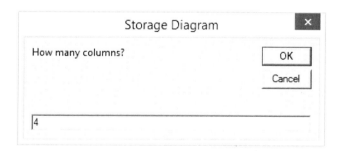

g) Press **Enter**.

You are prompted to enter the number of rows.

h) Type *5*

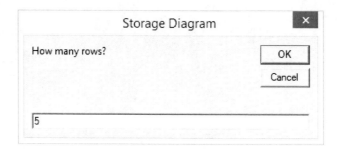

i) Press **Enter**.

You are prompted to identify what is stored in the bin.

j) Type *Box Dividers*.

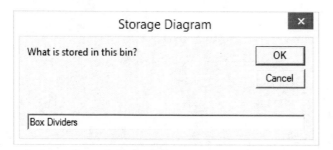

k) Press **Enter**.

You are prompted to identify where the bin is located.

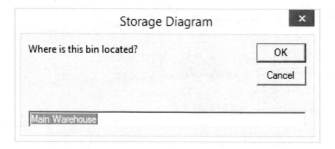

l) Select **OK** to accept the default value.

The diagram is created according to your specifications.

A1	B1	C1	D1
A2	B2	C2	D2
A3	B3	C3	D3
A4	B4	C4	D4
A5	B5	C5	D5

Bin Contents: Box Dividers
Bin Location: Main Warehouse

At this point, a user could enter the specific names of items within each compartment.

11. Examine the completed macro.

a) On the ribbon, if necessary, select the **DEVELOPER** tab. In the **Code** group, select **Visual Basic**.
The VBA programming editor is shown.

b) Examine the **BinStorage** macro code.
The simple macro you recorded has been expanded considerably. The code does the following:

- Various input values entered by the user are validated. If improper values are provided, messages are shown to the user, and the macro ends (Exit Sub).
- Various calculations are performed before the boxes are drawn.
- Two "For" loops repeat the box-drawing commands until boxes for all columns and rows are drawn.
- Title text is added, and numerous lines of code format individual attributes of the text, such as font size and text alignment.

12. Look up information regarding Visual Basic code.

a) Scroll to find the **DrawRectangle** command and select the word **DrawRectangle**.

This statement appears in the second half of the code listing.
b) Press **F1** to get help on the selected command.

Documentation on the selected command loads from the web.

c) Scroll to examine what is provided in the documentation.

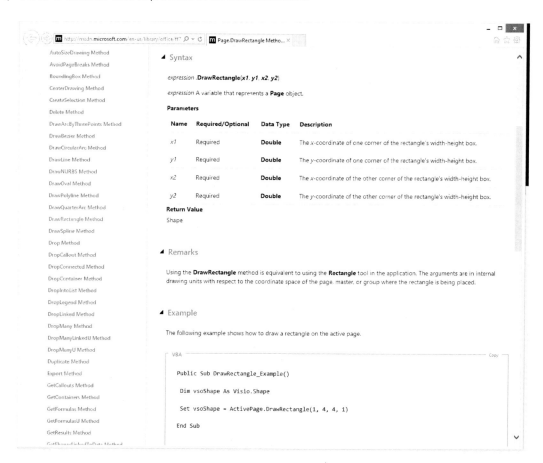

Documentation includes rules on writing a DrawRectangle statement (syntax), remarks on using the DrawRectangle, and a code example. This site serves as a comprehensive VBA reference. Many other VBA programming language elements are described in this documentation.

d) Close the web browser to return to the **Microsoft Visual Basic for Applications** window.

e) In the **Microsoft Visual Basic for Applications** window, select **File→Close and Return to Visio**.

13. Save the document in the **C:\091115Data\Leveraging Development Tools** folder as *My Finished Macro Diagram.vsdm*

14. Close all documents but leave Visio running.

TOPIC B

Modify ShapeSheets

Although Visio's powerful layout, formatting, and macro programming capabilities make it an extremely powerful drawing tool, there is even more power behind Visio. Imagine if you could take something such as the data processing capabilities of an Excel spreadsheet and apply it to the drawing environment of Visio. That's essentially what ShapeSheets do. By using ShapeSheets, you can create shapes that are intelligent and can interact with the page and other shapes around them.

ShapeSheets

A *ShapeSheet* is a spreadsheet that contains information about a Visio object. ShapeSheets govern how an object looks and behaves. Every object in Visio—not just shapes—has a ShapeSheet. When you select a shape and then select the **Show ShapeSheet** icon on the **DEVELOPER** tab, Visio opens the shape's ShapeSheet as a new window below the Visio window.

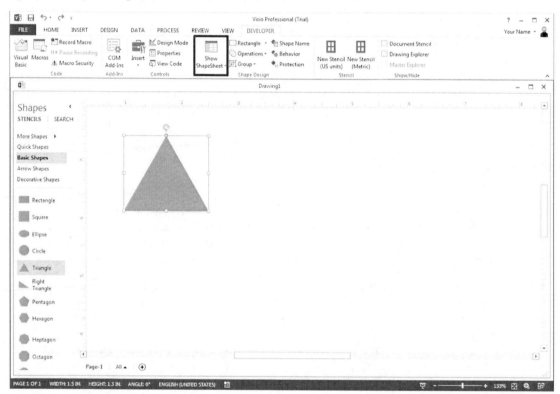

Figure 4-7: The Show ShapeSheet command.

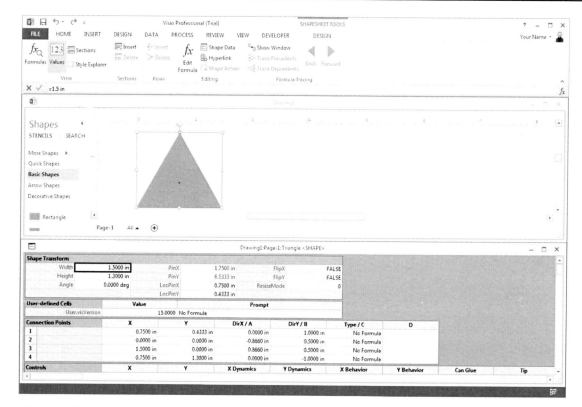

Figure 4-8: An open ShapeSheet.

A ShapeSheet contains many sections, rows, cells, and functions. If you select a cell in the ShapeSheet, Visio displays the formula or value it contains in an edit field below the ribbon. You can then change the formula or value in the edit field. Alternately, you can double-click a cell and change the formula or value directly in the cell.

> **Note:** You can also access the **Show ShapeSheet** command by right-clicking a shape.

> **Note:** The purpose of each ShapeSheet element isn't always obvious. However, Microsoft includes a complete ShapeSheet reference at **http://msdn.microsoft.com/en-us/library/office/ff765103.aspx**.

Types of ShapeSheets

You can access three kinds of the ShapeSheets from the **Show ShapeSheet** command:

- The **Shape** option opens the ShapeSheet for the selected shape. (This has the same effect as selecting the **Show ShapeSheet** icon.)
- The **Page** option opens the ShapeSheet for the current page.
- The **Document** option opens the ShapeSheet for the current drawing.

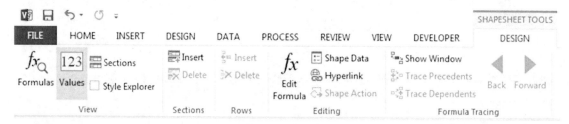

Figure 4-9: The options available from the Show ShapeSheet menu.

ShapeSheet Tools

When Visio shows a ShapeSheet, it also displays the **SHAPESHEET TOOLS | DESIGN** contextual tab. The commands on this tab enable you to change the selected ShapeSheet.

SHAPESHEET TOOLS | DESIGN *Figure 4-10: The SHAPESHEET TOOLS | DESIGN contextual tab.*

The commands on this tab enable you to make a number of changes to the ShapeSheet. The table below describes each command on the tab.

Group / Command	Description
**View	Formulas**	Shows formulas in cells.
**View	Values**	Shows values in cells.
**View	Sections**	Opens the **View Sections** dialog box so that you can hide and unhide sections of the ShapeSheet.
**View	Style Explorer**	Opens the **Style Explorer** window to the right of the **ShapeSheet** pane so that you can navigate through the layers of a style. If desired, you can float the **Style Explorer** window, or dock it below or to the left of the ShapeSheet window.
**Section	Insert**	Opens the **Insert Sections** dialog box so that you can add more sections to the ShapeSheet.
**Section	Delete**	Removes the selected section of the ShapeSheet.
**Row	Insert**	Adds a row above the selected row. This command isn't active unless you select a location where a row can be inserted.
**Row	Delete**	Removes the selected row of the ShapeSheet.
**Editing	Edit Formula**	Open the **Edit Formula** dialog box so that you can make changes to the formula of the selected cell.
**Editing	Shape Data**	Open the **Shape Data** dialog box so that you can define and change the data properties of a shape.

Group / Command	Description
Editing | Hyperlink	Open the **Hyperlink** dialog box so that you can define and change the hyperlinks associated with a shape.
Editing | Shape Action	Open the **Actions** dialog box so that you can define and change the actions associated with a shape. This command isn't active unless you select an actions row in the actions section of the ShapeSheet.
Formula Tracing | Show Window	Opens the **Formula Tracking** window to the right of the **ShapeSheet** pane so that you can navigate through the layers of a style. If desired, you can float the **Style Explorer** window or dock it below or left of the ShapeSheet window.
Formula Tracing | Trace Precedents	Shows the cells that are factored into the formula of the selected cell.
Formula Tracing | Trace Dependents	Shows the cells that are impacted by the formula of the selected cell.
Formula Tracing | Back	Moves to the previous cell you selected in the ShapeSheet.
Formula Tracing | Formula	Moves to the next cell you selected in the ShapeSheet.

 Access the Checklist tile on your LogicalCHOICE course screen for reference information and job aids on How to Modify ShapeSheets.

ACTIVITY 4-2
Modifying ShapeSheets

Before You Begin
Visio is running. The DEVELOPER tab is unhidden. No document is open.

Scenario
You are creating a template that you will use for various factory floor diagrams. The documents based on this template will vary in size, but they will always have an information box at the top that contains titling information, as shown.

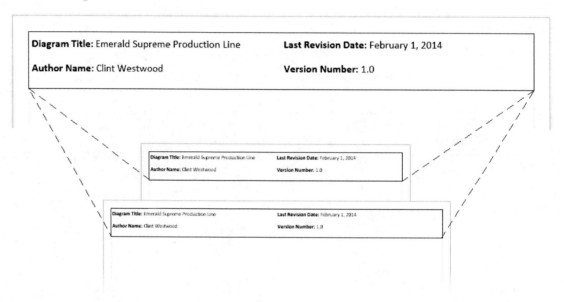

Ultimately, you want to have one drawing template that can be resized or oriented in landscape or portrait, as needed by the documentation team. The title box will be smart. When the page dimensions change, the box and the text boxes it contains will adjust their width and location so they always fit in the top of the page, nestled beneath and between the page margins.

---

1. Draw the border of the information box.
   a) Create a new Visio document based on the **Blank Drawing** template.
   b) On the **DESIGN** tab, in the **Page Setup** group, make sure that **Auto Size** is *not* selected.
   c) On the **HOME** tab, in the **Tools** group, select the **Rectangle** tool.
      Or you can press **Ctrl+8**, the keyboard shortcut, to select the **Rectangle** tool.

d) Just below the top margin and between the right and left margins, draw a rectangle that is about 1 inch tall.

Within this information box, each factory floor diagram will contain the diagram title, author name, last revision date, and version number.

e) On the **HOME** tab, in the **Tools** group, select **Pointer** tool.

Or you can press **Ctrl+1**, the keyboard shortcut to select the Pointer tool.

2. Examine how the box fails to resize and reposition itself.

a) On the **DESIGN** tab, in the **Page Setup** group, select **Orientation**.

Options are shown for **Portrait** and **Landscape**.

b) Select **Landscape**.

The wide dimension is now horizontal. The information box does not resize to fit and it is in the wrong location. Its position is always relative to the bottom margin of the page and its width is fixed.

c) Switch back to **Portrait** orientation.

d) On the **DESIGN** tab, in the **Page Setup** group, select **Size**, and select the **Legal** size.

Because the Legal sized page is taller and the location of the shape is measured up from the bottom of the page, the shape is not directly beneath the top margin.

e) Switch back to **Letter** size.

f) Consider the problem with this shape's default behavior.

You need this shape to be a bit smarter. The shape should:

• Always position itself beneath the top and left margins of the page.

• Always expand its width to the page's width (minus the amount taken by the left and right margins of the page).

• Always stay the same height.

3. Show the ShapeSheet for the rectangle.

a) Right-click the rectangle and select **Show ShapeSheet**.

Depending on your window layout and monitor size, the ShapeSheet window may now overlap your drawing window.

b) Click in the drawing window.

The ShapeSheet window may now be hidden behind your drawing window. This arrangement will be frustrating because you will need to work with both windows at the same time.

c) On the **VIEW** tab, in the **Window** group, select **Arrange All**.

The drawing and ShapeSheet windows are arranged side by side. While this is better, it will be easier to work with the ShapeSheet if the window is wider. Instead of arranging side by side, you can stack the two windows vertically.

d) While pressing the **Ctrl** key, on the **VIEW** tab, in the **Window** group, select **Arrange All**.

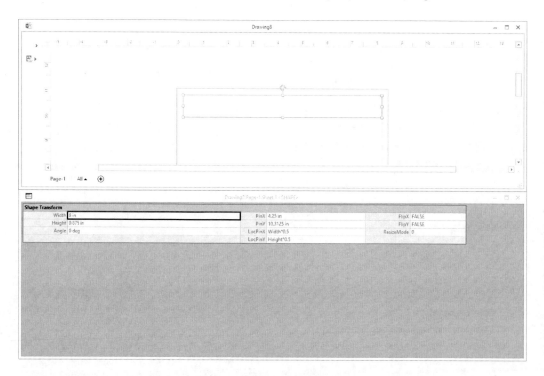

When **Ctrl** is pressed, this command arranges the windows stacked vertically. Your ShapeSheet may currently be showing more information than what is shown here.

e) In the ShapeSheet, right-click a blank area in the ShapeSheet and select **View Sections**.

The ShapeSheet contains a lot of information about the shape. It can be overwhelming to wade through all of the various sections just to find the values you want to work with. You can filter the sections to show only those you want to work with.

f) Select **None**.

Of those values that you are allowed to change, none of them are checked after you select None.

g) Check **Shape transform**.

This is the only section you will work with at this time.

h) Select **OK**.

Only the **Shape Transform** section is shown. In this section's cells, you can control the shape's behavior regarding width, height, angle, and various other attributes.

4. In the ShapeSheet, program the rectangle shape to fit the width between left and right margins.

a) In the ShapeSheet, examine the current value within the **Width** cell.

The width is currently hardcoded to be 7.5 inches.

b) In the **Width** cell, type the formula as shown and press **Enter**.

Shape Transform	
Width	=ThePage!PageWidth-ThePage!PageLeftMargin-ThePage!PageRightMargin

You must spell and capitalize the formula as shown.

In the cell, the first part of the formula may scroll of the left side as you type, which is okay. You can see the complete formula at the top of the screen, in the formula bar beneath the ribbon.

The formula begins with an equal sign to indicate that this value is not literal, but should be computed. This is similar to how an Excel spreadsheet formula is constructed.

The formula obtains the width between the margins by starting with the page width, and subtracting the left margin and right margin widths.

Because there are many different objects in a Visio document, you need to be specific about which object's properties you refer to. In this case, all three properties you include in the formula are properties of the current page. The prefix `ThePage!` identifies the current page object.

> **Note:** When you are programming shapes in the ShapeSheet, be careful not to resize or reposition shapes in the drawing, as this will overwrite the formulas.

5. In the ShapeSheet, program the pin settings to pin the shape to the top-left corner of the page.

a) Examine the pin settings.

PinX	4.25 in
PinY	10.3125 in
LocPinX	Width*0.5
LocPinY	Height*0.5

These settings identify how the shape is positioned or pinned on the page.

The **LocPinX** and **LocPinY** settings define the point within the shape that is anchored or pinned to the page. Currently, the shape is pinned from its center—halfway across its width (width times one half) and halfway up its height (height times one half).

The **PinX** and **PinY** settings identify where in the page the shape is pinned.

b) Select the **PinX** cell and press **Ctrl+E**.

The Edit Formula box provides a larger text area in which you can edit a formula. Because some cells are quite narrow, this view can be quite helpful when you are entering long formulas.

c) Revise the formula for **PinX** as shown.

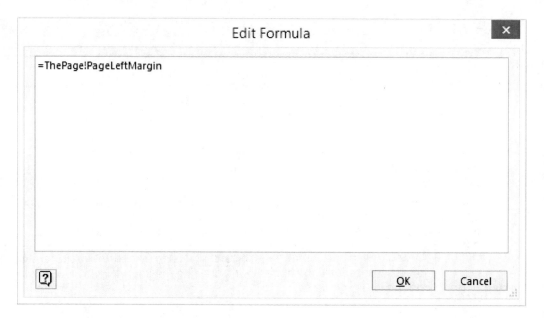

You will pin the shape to the page's left margin.

d) Select **OK**.

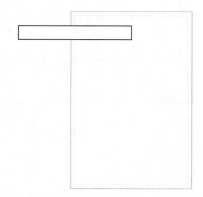

The center of the shape is now pinned to the left margin.

e) In the **PinY** cell, enter the formula *=ThePage!PageHeight-ThePage!PageTopMargin* and press **Enter**.

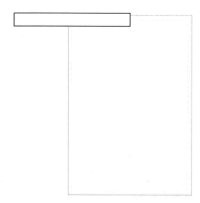

In the drawing, you can see that the center of the shape is now pinned to the top-left margin, and the LocPinX cell is selected in the ShapeSheet.

Now you need to adjust the pinning location within the shape. Instead of pinning the shape from its center, you can pin it from its top-left corner so it will nestle within the margins.

f) Press **Down Arrow** to select the **LocPinX** cell.

g) In the ShapeSheet, on the right edge of the PinX cell, drag the column divider to the right as shown, to create more room in the ShapeSheet to display the pin formulas.

You can adjust the column widths to provide more area for editing and viewing ShapeSheet cells.

6. In the ShapeSheet, program the rectangle shape to pin from its top-left corner rather than its center.

a) In the **LocPinX** cell, enter *0* and press **Down Arrow**.

The shape now pins from its left side.

The shape is still being pinned from its own vertical center.

b) Edit the formula in the **LocPinY** cell to *=Height* and press **Enter**.

The shape now pins from its top.

Since the Height value in the formula did not have the Page! prefix, it refers to the height of the shape itself (and not the height of the page). Because Visio uses coordinates that originate from the bottom of the page and the bottom of shapes, you have to offset LocPinY by the amount of the shape's height.

7. Test the shape's ability to adjust its position automatically.
    a) Click on the drawing to activate the drawing window.
    b) On the **DESIGN** tab, in the **Page Setup** group, select **Orientation**.
    c) Select **Landscape**.

The wide dimension is now horizontal. The information box resizes and repositions, due to its Width and Pin formulas. The Height remains fixed, as it contains a fixed value.

    d) Switch back to **Portrait** orientation.

e) On the **DESIGN** tab, in the **Page Setup** group, select **Size**, and select the **Legal** size.

The box adjusts to the new layout. (You may need to scroll to see the rest of the page.)

f) Switch back to **Letter** size.

If you were to develop this page further, you could place other shapes within this rectangle and program them to also adjust their size and location based on the page's dimensions.

8. Protect the ShapeSheet formulas.

a) In the drawing, select the rectangle shape.

Be very careful not to move the shape, as doing so will overwrite formulas you wrote to set its position.

b) On the **DEVELOPER** tab, in the **Shape Design** group, select **Protection**.

You can protect various attributes of the shape from being changed.

c) Select the protection options as shown.

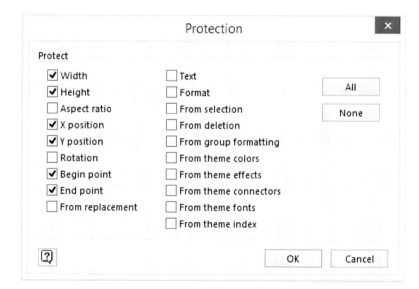

d) Select **OK**.

Slashes appear within the rectangles selection handles, showing that they are protected. Although these settings can be modified by typing new values into the ShapeSheet, these values now can't be overwritten by a user making modifications to the drawing.

9. Identify attributes that can be controlled through ShapeSheets.

a) Double-click the title bar of the ShapeSheet to activate and expand its window.

b) Right-click the large gray area in the ShapeSheet.

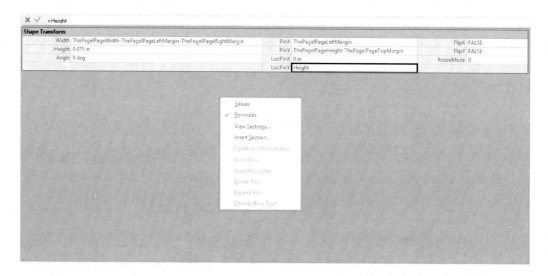

c) Select **View Sections**.

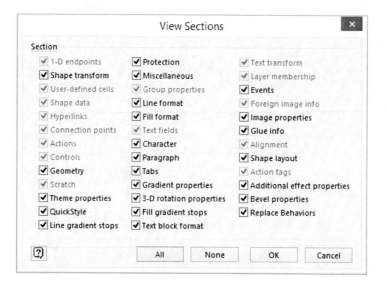

d) Select **All** and then select **OK**.

All of the available sections of shape attributes are shown in the ShapeSheet. Most of these values can be edited and controlled through ShapeSheet functions or VBA macros. Much of the power and flexibility of Visio lies in the capability provided by ShapeSheets. Visio shapes can be programmed to update themselves based on the layout of the page they are in, attributes of other shapes they are associated with, the time of day, and numerous other conditions.

e) Scroll through the ShapeSheet to get a sense of the variety of settings available in the ShapeSheet.

10. Save the document.

a) On the **VIEW** tab, in the **Window** group, select **Switch Windows** and select the drawing window.

b) Save the document in the **C:\091115Data\Leveraging Development Tools** folder with the file type **Visio Drawing (*.vsdx)** as *My Smart Shape.vsdx*

TOPIC C

Build Advanced Shapes

Shape design commands are the another development tool with which you should be familiar. Shape design commands enable you to build complex shapes—especially vector graphics that can be scaled without image degradation.

Drawing Tools

You can access six drawing tools from the **Shape Design** group of the **DEVELOPER** tab. All of them are them are contained in a **Drawing Tools** drop-down menu. The icon and name indicating the **Drawing Tools** menu changes depending on which tool you select. You can also find the **Drawing Tools** menu on the **HOME** tab.

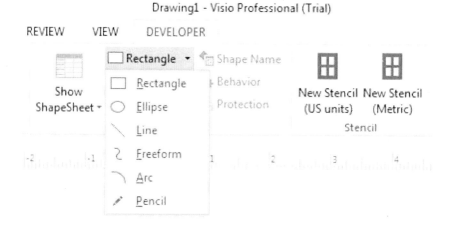

Figure 4-11: The Drawing Tools menu.

The following table lists what you can draw with each tool.

Tool	What It Can Draw	Tips
Rectangle	Squares or rectangles	To draw a square, press and hold the **Shift** key as you draw.
Ellipse	Circles or ellipses (also known as an ovals)	To draw a circle, press and hold the **Shift** key as you draw.
Line	Straight lines	To draw a line that is perfectly horizontal, vertical, or diagonal, hold the **Shift** key as you draw.
Freeform	Any shape as a continuous path composed of several line segments	
Arc	Elliptical arcs	
Pencil	Straight lines or circular arcs	

Shape Operations

The **Shape Design** group of the **DEVELOPER** tab also contains the **Operations** menu—which enables you do a number of useful things to selected shapes. This menu isn't active unless you select at least one shape.

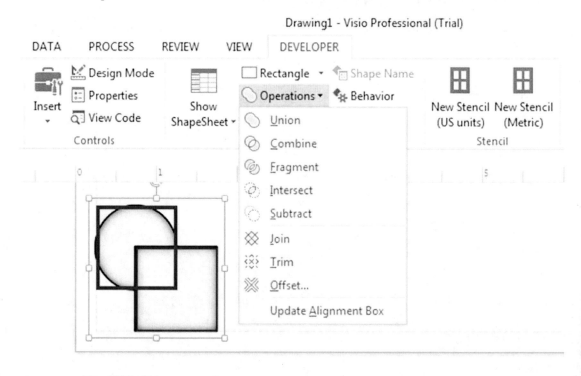

Figure 4–12: The Operations menu.

The following table describes each operation.

Operation	Description	Example
None	Original shapes	

Operation	Description	Example
Union	Creates a new shape from the perimeter of two or more overlapping shapes	
Combine	Creates a new shape that cuts out the overlapping portion of two or more shapes	
Fragment	Divides two or more shapes into smaller parts based on intersections and overlaps	
Intersect	Creates a new shape from the overlapping area of two or more shapes	
Subtract	Creates a new shape by removing from the primary shape the overlapping area with other shapes	

Operation	Description	Example
Join	Joins individual line segments into one or more continuous paths	
Trim	Creates new shapes by dividing selected shapes at their intersections	
Offset	Shows the **Offset** dialog box, from which you can create a set of new lines that parallel the selected shapes	

Shape Groups

The **Shape Design** group of the **DEVELOPER** tab also contains the **Group** drop-down menu. If you select two or more shapes, then select the **Group**→**Group** command, Visio combines the shapes into a group and treats them as a single shape. This enables you to easily move and format all of the shapes in the group.

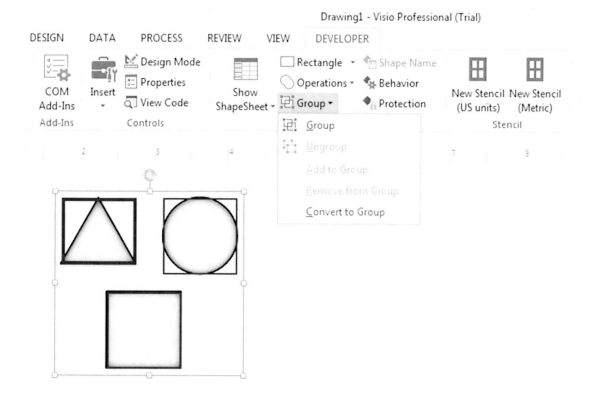

Figure 4-13: The Group menu.

Other Commands in the Group Menu

The **Group** drop-down menu contains several other commands that you can apply to a shape group:

- Use the **Ungroup** command to break a group into individual shapes.
- Use the **Add to Group** command to add a selected shape to a selected group.
- Use the **Remove from Group** command to ungroup a selected shape from the group.
- Use the **Convert to Group** command to transform a pasted or imported metafile graphic into a group.

 Note: You can also access the **Group** command by selecting two or more shapes and then right-clicking. Similarly, you can access the **Ungroup** command by selecting a group and then right-clicking.

 Note: You can modify an individual shape in a group without removing it from the group. Simply select the group, then select the shape you want to change.

Shape Names

If you select the **Shape Name** command, Visio opens the **Shape Name** dialog box—which allows you to change the name of a shape. You can also add or edit other shape attributes.

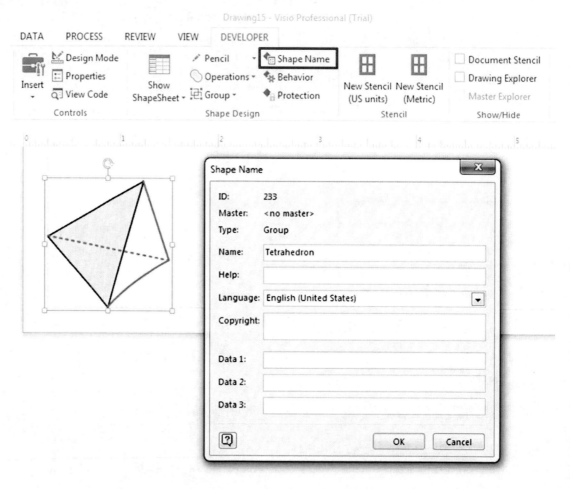

Figure 4-14: The Shape Name dialog box.

Shape Behaviors

If you select the **Behavior** command, Visio opens the **Behavior** dialog box—which allows you to change the interaction properties of a shape. This is a complex dialog box with over two dozen options.

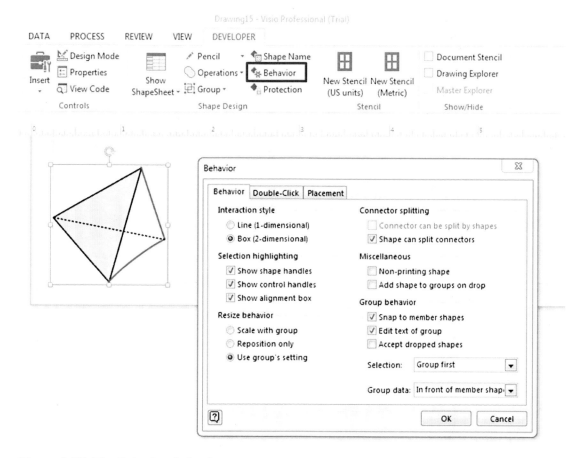

Figure 4-15: The Behavior dialog box.

Shape Protection

If you select the **Protection** command, Visio opens the **Protection** dialog box—which allows you to lock a number of shape properties and thus prevent undesired changes.

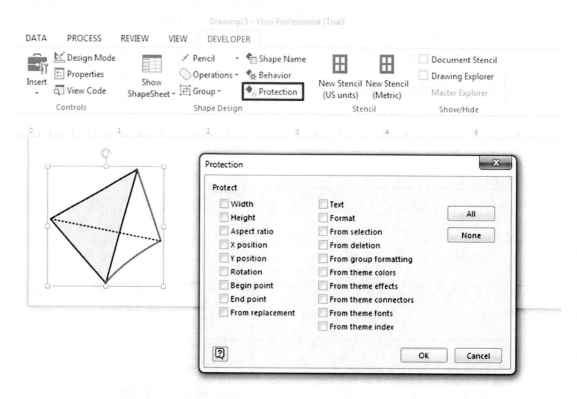

Figure 4-16: The Protection dialog box.

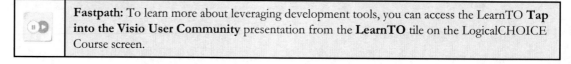

Fastpath: To learn more about leveraging development tools, you can access the LearnTO **Tap into the Visio User Community** presentation from the **LearnTO** tile on the LogicalCHOICE Course screen.

Access the Checklist tile on your LogicalCHOICE course screen for reference information and job aids on How to Build Advanced Shapes.

ACTIVITY 4-3
Building Advanced Shapes

Before You Begin
Visio Professional 2013 is open.

Scenario
Mary Kaplan, vice president for marketing, asked you to create a flowchart that depicts the olive oil production process from grove to store. You need an abstract olive shape, but a search of the stencils doesn't yield any useful results. So, you decide to create a custom shape.

---

1. Create a new, blank drawing from the **Blank Drawing** template.

2. Draw an oval.
   a) On the ribbon, select the **DEVELOPER** tab.
   b) In the **Shape Design** group, select the down arrow beside the **Rectangle** to open the **Drawing Tools** drop-down menu.

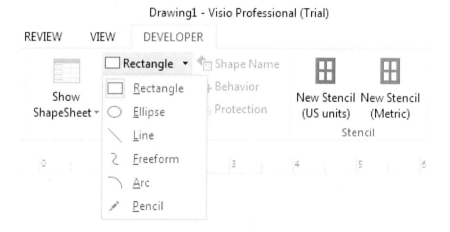

   c) Select the **Ellipse** tool.
   d) Move the mouse pointer to the drawing page.
   e) Press and hold the left mouse button to set the starting point for the ellipse.
      It doesn't matter where on the drawing you start the circle.

f) Drag the mouse pointer right and slightly down to trace an ellipse that is about 3 inches wide and 2 inches high.

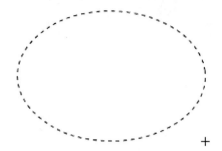

g) Release the left mouse button to set the ending point for the ellipse.

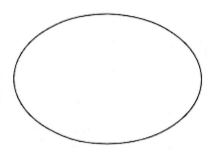

3. Draw a circle.

Notice that the **Ellipse** tool is still active.

a) Press and hold the left mouse button to set the starting point for the circle.

It doesn't matter where on the drawing you start the circle.

b) Press and hold the **Shift** key so that you can draw a perfect circle.

c) Drag the mouse pointer right and down to trace a circle that is about 1 inch wide and 1 inch high.

The diagonal guideline indicates that you are tracing a perfect circle.

d) Release the left mouse button to set the ending point for the circle.

4. Change the **Fill** and **Line** colors of the shapes so that you can see them better.

a) Press the **Ctrl** and **A** keys to select both shapes.

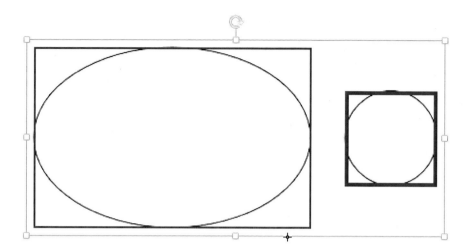

b) On the ribbon, select the **HOME** tab.

c) In the **Shape Styles** group, select the **Fill** drop-down arrow. Fill ▾

d) From the **Fill** drop-down menu, in the **Recent Colors** section, select the green color swatch (R0, G100, B0).

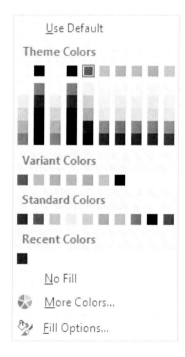

This is the Emerald Epicure green you used earlier in the course. If the Emerald Epicure green color swatch is missing from the **Recent Colors** section, select **More Colors** and in the **Colors** dialog box, set **Red** to *0*, **Green** to *100*, **Blue** to *0*, and select **OK**.

e) In the **Shape Styles** group, select the **Line** drop-down arrow. Line ▾

f) From the **Line** drop-down menu, in the **Recent Colors** section, select the green color swatch (R0, G100, B0).

g) Press the **Esc** key to deselect both shapes.
   Both shapes have a green fill and outline.

5. Overlap the two shapes.
   a) Select **HOME→Tools→Pointer Tool**.
   b) Drag the circle on top of the ellipse.
   c) Put the circle near the right side of the ellipse.

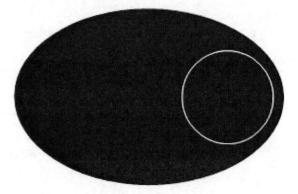

6. Apply an operation to the shapes.
   a) Select the ellipse, press the **Ctrl** key, select the circle, and release the **Ctrl** key.

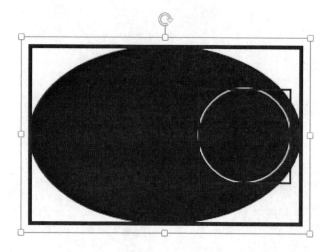

   b) On the ribbon, select the **DEVELOPER** tab.

c) In the **Shape Design** group, select **Operations→Subtract**.

Visio subtracts the circle from the ellipse.

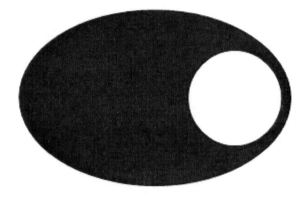

7. Name the shape.
   a) In the **Shape Design** group, select the **Shape Name** command.
   b) In the **Shape Name** dialog box, select the text in the **Name** field and type *My Olive*

c) Select the **Copyright** field and type *Emerald Epicure*

d) Select **OK** to close the dialog box.

8. Add the olive shape to **My EE Stencil**.

a) In the **Shapes** window, select **More Shapes→My Shapes→My EE Stencil**. The **My EE Stencil** appears in the **Shapes** window.

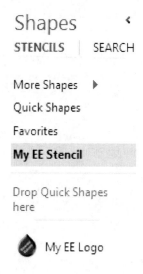

b) Drag the olive shape to the **Shapes** window and put it below **My EE Logo**.
Visio opens a dialog box asking if you want to edit the stencil.

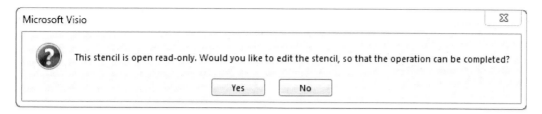

c) Select **Yes**.
Visio adds the olive as a new master shape in the **My EE Stencil**.

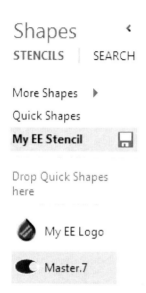

d) Right-click the new master shape. From the shortcut menu, select **Rename Master**. Replace the
default name by typing *My Olive* and press the **Esc** key.

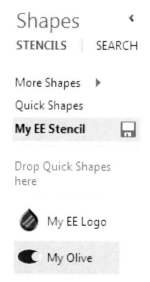

e) Select the **Save** icon to save the changes to **My EE Stencil**. My EE Stencil 💾

The **Save** icon changes to a red asterisk. My EE Stencil   *

9. Close the blank drawing. You don't need to save it.

Summary

In this lesson, you became familiar with some of Visio's developer tools so that you can be a power user. You created macros to automate repetitive tasks. You modified ShapeSheets to make shapes more intelligent. Finally, you built advanced shapes that can be scaled.

Do you anticipate recording macros in your work environment? Why or why not?

What advanced custom shapes might you need to create in your work environment?

 Note: Check your LogicalCHOICE Course screen for opportunities to interact with your classmates, peers, and the larger LogicalCHOICE online community about the topics covered in this course or other topics you are interested in. From the Course screen you can also access available resources for a more continuous learning experience.

5 | Sharing Drawings

Lesson time: 1 hour, 5 minutes

Lesson Objectives

In this lesson, you will share drawings. You will:

- Save and share drawings on Microsoft OneDrive.

- Review drawings.

- Insert drawings into other Microsoft Office files.

- Convert Visio drawings into other file formats

- Print drawings.

Lesson Introduction

Now that you know how to design informative and appealing drawings, you need to be familiar with the many ways you can share those drawings with others.

TOPIC A

Save and Share Drawings with OneDrive

Effectively using cloud-based file sharing services is essential in today's business environment—especially when you're working on drawings with clients and contractors who don't have access to your company's network.

OneDrive

Microsoft® OneDrive® is a cloud-based storage service. When you save your Visio drawings (and other files) to your OneDrive account, you can access them on any Internet-connected device. If you wish, you can also share your drawings (and other files) with others. OneDrive comes with your Microsoft account. You can store up to 7 GB of data for free. You can buy more space if you need it.

Figure 5-1: OneDrive viewed with a web browser.

> **Note:** Visit **http://windows.microsoft.com/en-us/skydrive/** to learn more about OneDrive.

Options for Sharing Drawings on OneDrive

After you save a Visio drawing on OneDrive, you can share the drawing with your colleagues by sending them an email invitation from the **Share** tab of Visio's **Backstage**. When preparing the invitation, you need to make a couple of choices:

- **Do you want them to be able to edit the drawing, or just view it?** If want your colleagues to use Visio's comment feature or actually modify the drawing, you'll want to select the **Can edit** option. If you don't want you colleagues to add comments or make changes, select the **Can view** option.

- **Do you want to require them to sign in to their OneDrive account to view or edit the drawing?** Checking the **Require user to sign in before accessing document** check box provides an extra level of security to your drawings. You definitely should check this box if you are allowing colleagues to edit the drawing.

Figure 5-2: Inviting someone to edit a drawing saved in OneDrive.

Visio and Visio Viewer

If you invite your colleagues to edit your Visio drawings, be aware that they must have Visio 2013 installed on their computers. If you invite your colleagues to view your Visio drawings, they must have Visio 2013 or Visio 2013 Viewer installed on their computers.

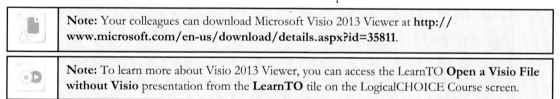

Note: Your colleagues can download Microsoft Visio 2013 Viewer at **http://www.microsoft.com/en-us/download/details.aspx?id=35811**.

Note: To learn more about Visio 2013 Viewer, you can access the LearnTO **Open a Visio File without Visio** presentation from the **LearnTO** tile on the LogicalCHOICE Course screen.

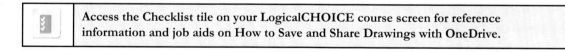

Access the Checklist tile on your LogicalCHOICE course screen for reference information and job aids on How to Save and Share Drawings with OneDrive.

ACTIVITY 5-1
Saving and Sharing Drawings with OneDrive

Data File

C:\091115Data\Sharing Drawings\Cinnamon Oil Project Gantt Chart Final.vsdx

Before You Begin

Visio is open.

Scenario

Emerald Epicure has contracted with Mixed Messages Media (MMM) to design and develop the new cinnamon oil advertising campaign. You're collaborating with another graphic artist, Jennifer Gonzalez, at MMM. She recommends using OneDrive to share files between EE and MMM. You agree. To begin, she asks you put the Cinnamon Oil Project Gantt Chart on OneDrive.

1. Verify that Visio is connected to OneDrive.
   a) On the ribbon, select the **FILE** tab.
   b) On the **Backstage**, select **Open**.
   c) On the **Open** screen, verify that your **OneDrive** account is listed.

   At the beginning of the course, when you signed in to Visio with your Microsoft account, Visio automatically connected to your OneDrive.

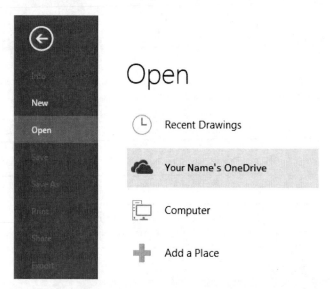

> **Note:** If you wish to connect Visio to another OneDrive account that you own, select **Add a Place→OneDrive**. In the **Add a service** dialog box, type the email address associated with the OneDrive account and select **Next**. In the **Sign in** dialog box, type the password associated with the OneDrive account and select **Sign in**. On the **Open** screen, the additional OneDrive will be listed.

2. Open the Gantt chart.
   a) On the **Open** screen, select **Computer→Browse**.

b) In the **Open** dialog box, navigate to the **C:\091115Data\Sharing Drawings** folder and double-click
   Cinnamon Oil Project Gantt Chart Final.vsdx.
   Visio opens the Gantt chart.

3. Save the Gantt chart to OneDrive.
   a) On the ribbon, select the **FILE** tab.
   b) On the **Backstage**, select **Save As**.
   c) On the **Save As** screen, select your **OneDrive** and the **Browse** button.

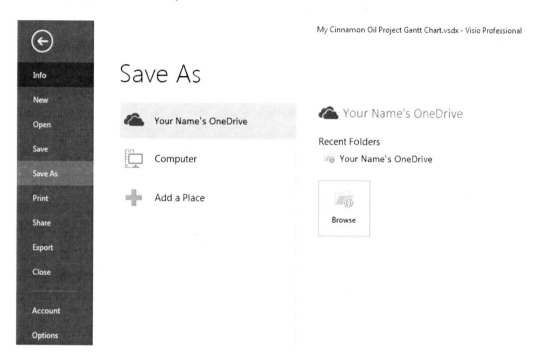

d) In the **Save As** dialog box, select the **New folder** command.

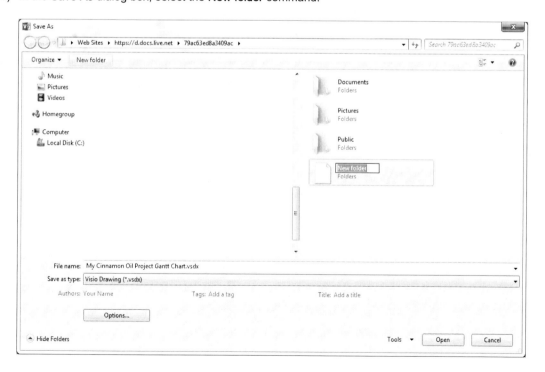

e) In the new folder name field, type *EE-MMM Shared Folder* and press **Enter**.

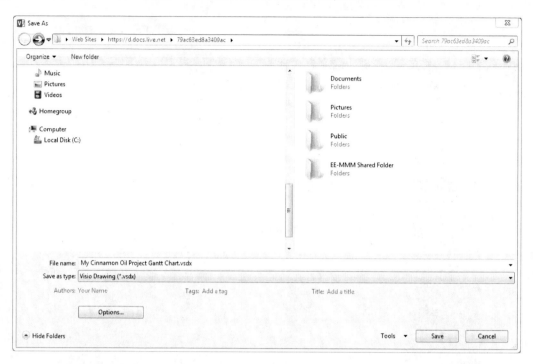

f) Double-click **EE-MMM Shared Folder**.
g) In the **File name** field, review the name of the file.

   You don't need to change the file name.
h) Select the **Save** button.
i) Visio saves the drawing to OneDrive.

4. Share the Gantt chart with Jennifer.
   a) On the ribbon, select the **FILE** tab.
   b) On the **Backstage**, select **Share**.
   c) On the **Share** screen, verify that the **Invite People** option is selected.
   d) In the **Type names or e-mail address** field, type *jennifer.gonzalez@mmm.tld*
   e) To the right pf Jennifer's email address, verify that **Can edit** rather then **Can view** is selected.

f) Verify that **Require user to sign in before accessing document** is checked.

This option provides better security for confidential drawings.

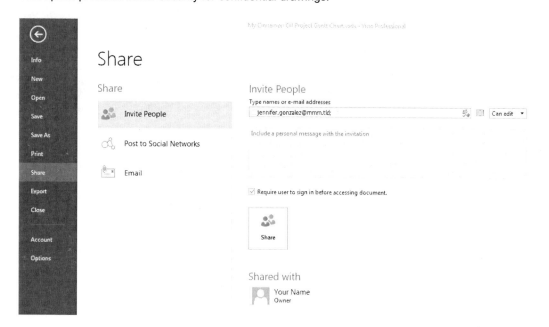

g) Select the **Share** button.

Visio sends the sharing invitation and adds Jennifer's email address to the list of people with whom you are sharing the drawing.

Shared with

Your Name
Owner

jennifer.gonzalez@mmm.tld
Can edit

5. Exit the **Backstage** and close the drawing.

TOPIC B

Review Drawings

Team work is one of the keys to great products and services. This is also true when creating Visio diagrams. Feedback from peers can make a drawing better, and approval by superiors is essential. Sometimes your work will be reviewed by others; other times you will review the work of others. Visio contains a valuable set of commenting tools.

The REVIEW Tab

The **REVIEW** tab on the ribbon contains three commands that enable you to add comments on drawings created by others:

- **New Comment**. This command adds a new comment to the drawing page or the selected shape.
- **Comments Pane**. This command opens the **Comments** pane.
- **Ink**. This command opens the **INK TOOLS** contextual tab.

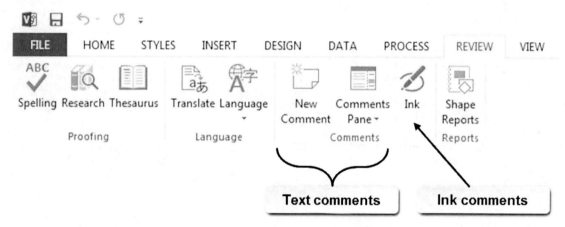

Figure 5–3: The REVIEW tab.

Comments and Replies

If no shape is selected when you select the **New Comment** command, Visio adds a new comment to the entire drawing page. If a shape or group of shapes is selected when you select the **New Comment** commands, Visio adds a new comment to the shape or group. Because you are signed in to Visio with your Microsoft account, you are identified as the person who added the comment.

When you first create a new comment, Visio displays it in a pop-up box. If you deselect the pop-up box, Visio collapses the comment and shows a comment icon in the top left corner of the drawing or adjacent to the shape or group to which the comment was applied. Select the comment icon to expand the pop-up box.

If you add more than one comment to the whole drawing, a shape, or a group, Visio displays all of the comments for the object in a single pop-up box. Below each comment is a **Reply** field, which allows other reviewers or the author to respond to your comment. This is very useful when the author is revising the drawing; he or she can reply that the suggested change was made or explain why the suggested changes was not made.

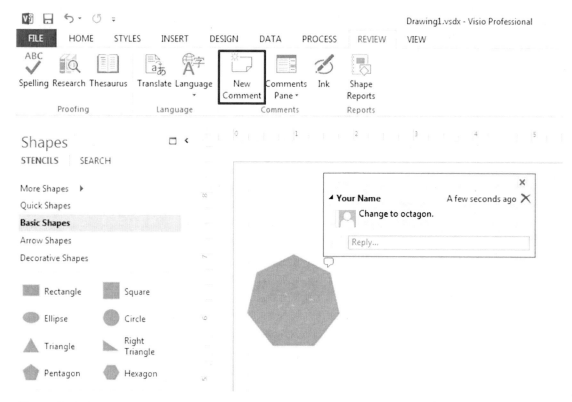

Figure 5-4: A new text comment.

 Note: Another method to add a new comment is to right-click on the drawing page, a shape, or a group and, from the shortcut menu, select **Add Comment**.

The Comments Pane

When you select the **Comments Pane** command on the **REVIEW** tab, Visio displays all comments in a docked pane at the right side of the screen.

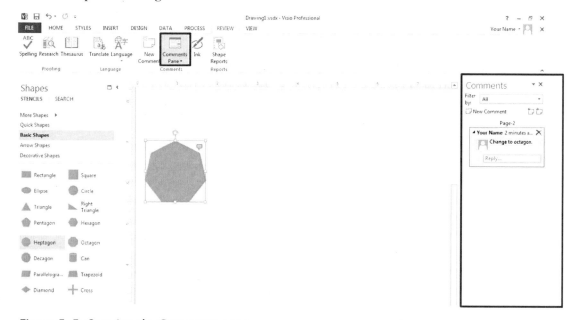

Figure 5-5: Opening the Comments pane.

The following table explains the commands you can perform in this window.

Command	Use
Filter by	Filter comments. The options are: • **All** • **Page** • **Recent** • **Collapsed** • **Expanded** You can also filter by commenter.
New Comment	Add a new comment to the selected object.
Previous	Go the previous comment in the pane.
Next	Go the next comment in the pane.

Ink Markup

When you select the **Ink** command on the **REVIEW** tab, Visio displays the **INK TOOLS** contextual tab. This tab contains a number of commands that enable you to add handwritten comments to a drawing. Ink comments are generally made with a tablet and stylus system. Although you can make ink comments with a mouse, it's more effort than it's worth.

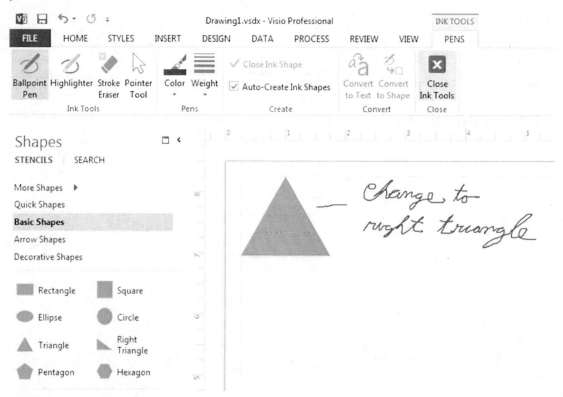

Figure 5-6: An ink markup.

This table describes the primary commands on the **INK TOOLS** tab.

Command	Use
Ballpoint Pen	Draw thin lines like a pen. This option is designed for handwriting.

Command	Use
Highlighter	Draw thick lines as with a highlighter.
Stroke Eraser	Select pen or highlighter marks you want to erase.
Pointer Tool	Select pen or highlighter marks you want to move or resize.
Color	Change the color of pen or highlighter marks. When you select this command, Visio displays a color gallery similar to those you've encountered previously.
Weight	Change the thickness of pen or highlighter marks. When you select this command, Visio displays a line gallery similar to those you've encountered previously. If the **Pen Pressure** option is checked, Visio increases the thickness of a line the harder you press on the stylus.
Close Ink Tools	Closes the **INK TOOLS** contextual tab.

 Note: Once you add an ink comment to a drawing, Visio treats it like any other shape.

 Note: Visio doesn't list ink comments on the **Comments** pane.

 Access the Checklist tile on your LogicalCHOICE course screen for reference information and job aids on How to Review Drawings.

ACTIVITY 5–2
Reviewing Drawings

Data File

C:\091115Data\Sharing Drawings\Media Mix Analysis Cinnamon Oil.vsdx

Before You Begin

Visio is open.

Scenario

Jennifer Gonzalez at Mixed Messages Media drafted a marketing mix analysis for the cinnamon oil advertising project and asked you to provide some feedback.

---

1. Open the drawing.
   a) On the ribbon, select the **FILE** tab.
   b) On the **Backstage**, select **Open→Computer→Browse**.
   c) In the **Open** dialog box, navigate to the **C:\091115Data\Sharing Drawings** folder and double-click **Media Mix Analysis Cinnamon Oil.vsdx**.
      Visio opens the drawing.

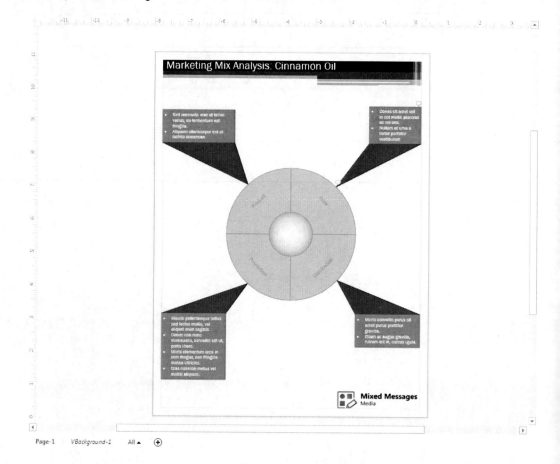

2. Add text comments to the drawing.

    a) On the drawing, select the large circle.
       This group consists of several shapes.
    b) On the ribbon, select the **REVIEW** tab.
    c) Select the **New Comment** command.
    d) In the comment field, type *Increase font size* and press the **Esc** key.

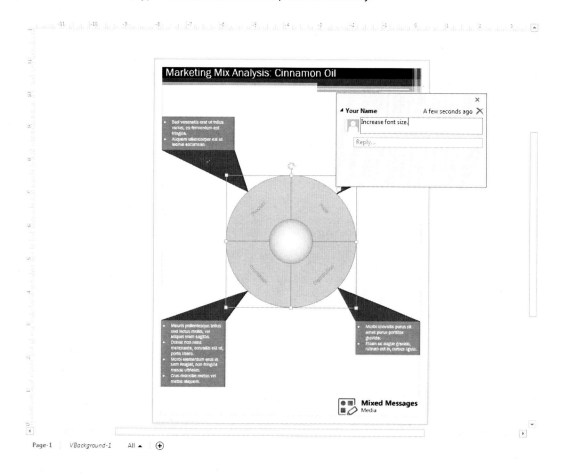

    e) Notice the comment icon near the upper right of the larger circle.

f) Right-click the large circle and, from the shortcut menu, select the **Add Comment** option.

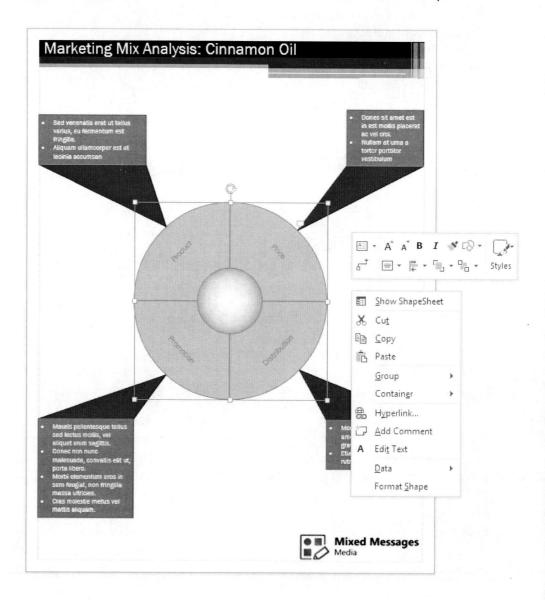

g) In the second comment field, type *Make each sector a different color* and press **Esc**.

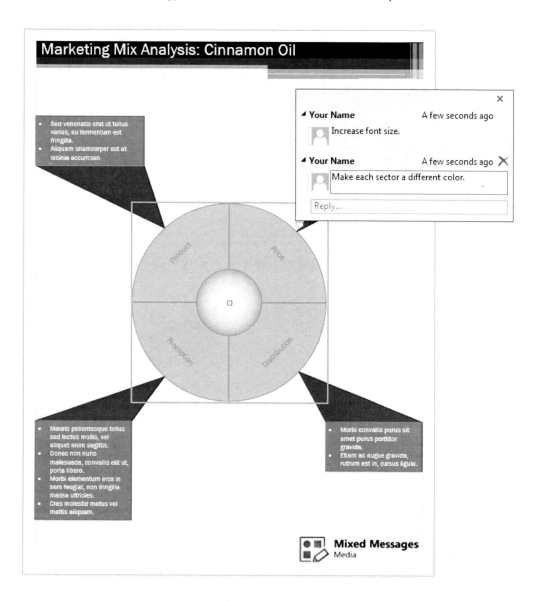

h) On the **REVIEW** tab, in the **Comments** group, select the **Comments Pane** command.
i) In the **Comments** pane, select the **New Comment** command.

j) In the third comment field, type *Change color of small circle to improve contrast with text* and press the **Esc** key.

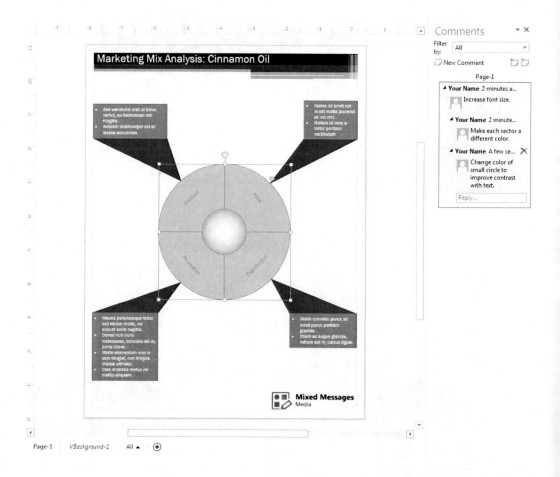

3. Save the drawing in **C:\091115Data\Sharing Drawings** as *My Media Mix Analysis Cinnamon Oil.vsdx*

4. Close the drawing.

TOPIC C

Insert Drawings into Other Office Files

Visio drawings often aren't stand-alone products. Frequently they are intended for use in Microsoft Word® documents, Microsoft PowerPoint® presentations, or other Microsoft Office files. This topic shows you two methods for putting Visio diagrams into other files.

Copy and Paste Options

Copy and paste is one method for putting Visio drawings into Word documents, PowerPoint slides, and other Microsoft Office files. After you copy all or part of a drawing in Visio, paste it in to the receiving file by using the **Paste Special** command. Each program gives you several **Paste Special** options.

PowerPoint 2013

Word 2013

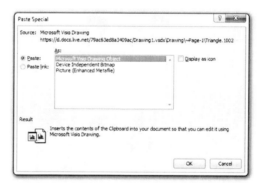

Figure 5–7: Options for inserting a copied Visio drawing into a PowerPoint presentation or Word document by using Paste Special.

This table describes each paste option.

Paste Option	Description
Microsoft Visio Drawing Object	Pastes the drawing as a Visio object. If you double-click the object in Word or PowerPoint, it will open in Visio so that you can edit it.
Device Independent Bitmap	Pastes the drawing as a raster graphic that contains a color table.
Bitmap	Pastes the drawing as a raster graphic.
Picture (Enhanced Metafile)	Pastes the drawing as a vector graphic.
Picture (Windows Metafile)	Pastes the drawing as a vector graphic. This is a legacy format that is rarely used today.

Insert Object Options

Inserting an OLE object is the second method for putting Visio drawings into Word documents, PowerPoint slides, and other Microsoft Office files. This method imports the drawing into the target file as an *Object Linking and Embedding (OLE)* object.

To use this method in either Word 2013 and Visio 2013, select the **INSERT** tab on the ribbon and then select the **Object** command. Visio will open an Object dialog box with two tabs. The first tab enables you to insert a new, blank Visio or other Office file into the target file. The second tab enables you to insert an existing Visio or other Office file into the target file. This tab has two import check boxes—**Link to file** and **Display as icon**. The following table explains the checked and unchecked state of each check box.

Check Box	Checked	Unchecked
Link to file	Windows establishes a persistent link between the target file and the original Visio drawing. Double-clicking the Visio drawing in the target file opens the original Visio drawing. Any changes made in the original Visio drawing will be reflected in the target file.	Windows simply inserts a copy of the original Visio drawing into the target document. This is essentially identical to the **Paste Special→Microsoft Visio Drawing Object** option discussed earlier in this topic.
Display as icon	Windows inserts the Visio drawing as an icon into the source file. Double-clicking the icon opens the Visio drawing.	Windows inserts the Visio drawing as a graphic rendering. Double-clicking the icon opens the Visio drawing.

Figure 5–8: Inserting a Visio drawing into a PowerPoint presentation or Word document.

> Access the Checklist tile on your LogicalCHOICE course screen for reference information and job aids on How to Insert Drawings into Other Office Files.

ACTIVITY 5-3
Inserting Drawings into Other Office Files

Data File

C:\091115Data\Sharing Drawings\Media Mix Analysis Cinnamon Oil Final.vsdx

Before You Begin

Visio is open.

Scenario

Jennifer Gonzalez at Mixed Messages Media appreciated your feedback and revised the marketing mix analysis drawing. In addition to the comments you made, Jennifer converted the drawing from portrait to landscape format. You shared the final drawing with Mary Kaplan, the vice president of marketing at Emerald Epicure. Mary asked you create a short Microsoft PowerPoint slide show that she can use to explain the drawing to the rest of the management team.

---

1. In Visio, open **C:\091115Data\Sharing Drawings\Media Mix Analysis Cinnamon Oil Final.vsdx**

2. Start a new slide show.
   a) Open PowerPoint 2013.
   b) On the **New** screen, select **Blank Presentation**.
   c) On the first slide, select **Click to add title** and type *Marketing Mix Analysis*
   d) Select **Click to add subtitle** and type *Cinnamon Oil*

e) On the ribbon, on the **HOME** tab, select the **New Slide** command.

New
Slide ▾

You don't need access the New Slide drop-down menu.

PowerPoint adds a new slide with the Title and Content layout.

f) On the second slide, select **Click to add title** and type *Media Mix Elements*

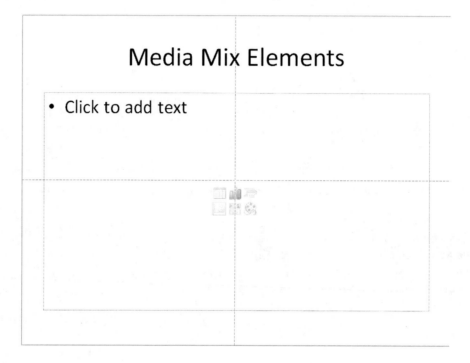

3. Copy the drawing in Visio.

a) Bring the Visio window to the foreground.

b) Press the **Ctrl** and **A** keys to select all the shapes in the drawing.

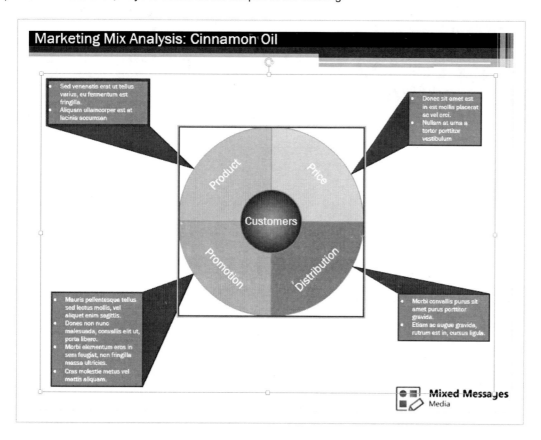

c) Press the **Ctrl** and **C** keys to copy the selected shapes.

4. Paste the drawing into PowerPoint.

a) Bring the PowerPoint window to the foreground.

b) Select the border of the content placeholder (rather than the interior of the content place holder).

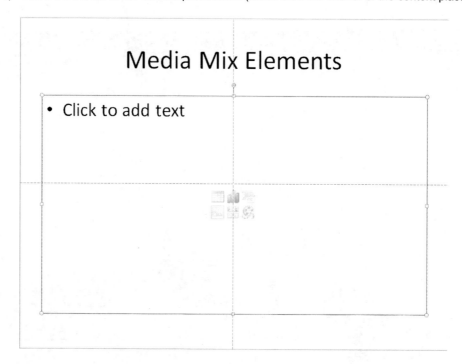

c) On the ribbon, on the **HOME** tab, select **Paste→Picture**.
   Windows pastes the drawing into the content placeholder as a non-editable picture.

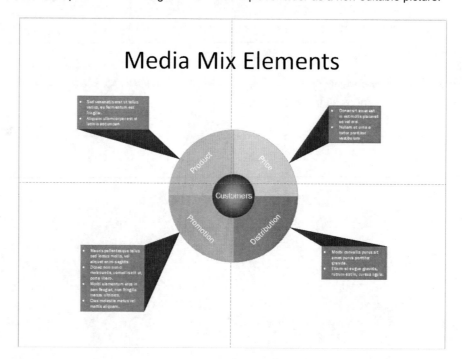

5. Save the slide show in the **C:\091115Data\Sharing Drawings** folder as *My Media Mix Analysis Cinnamon Oil Presentation.pptx*

6. Close PowerPoint.

7. Close **Media Mix Analysis Cinnamon Oil Final**.vsdx.

TOPIC D

Export Drawings

Unlike Microsoft Word and PowerPoint, Visio is a premium product that is not widely available. So, you often won't be able to share your drawing with others in Visio format. Instead, you'll need to export it another file format.

The Export Screen on the Backstage

The **Export** screen on Visio's **Backstage** enables you to convert your Visio drawings into a wide array of file formats. This enables you to choose the most appropriate format for using the drawing or sharing with others.

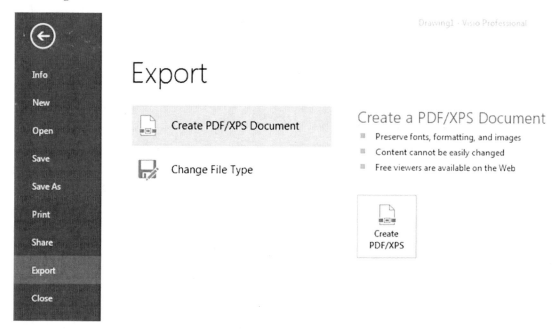

Figure 5-9: The Export screen on the Backstage.

PDF and XPS

You can use the **Create PDF/XPS Document** option to convert a drawing to either an Adobe® Portable Document Format (PDF) file or an XML Paper Specification (XPS) file. Because you are essentially printing the view to one of these file formats, you will find it helpful to use **Print Preview** and **Print Settings** on the **Print** screen before creating a PDF or XPS document.

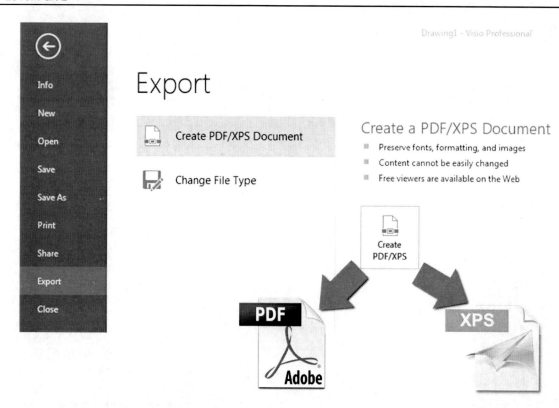

Figure 5-10: Exporting a drawing to PDF or XPS.

 Note: PDF is more widely used than XPS. The XPS format was originally developed by Microsoft as an alternative to PDF. PDFs can be opened with the free Adobe Reader®. XPS files can be opened with the XPS Viewer that is bundled with later versions of Windows®.

Visio Drawing Formats

In earlier lessons, you learned the difference between Visio shape, stencil, and template file formats. You also learned the difference between macro-enabled and macro-free Visio file formats. On the **Export** screen, you can choose to save your drawing in one of the four Visio file formats discussed earlier.

Export

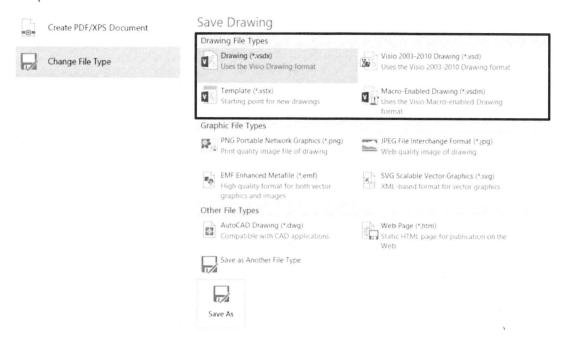

Figure 5-11: Exporting a drawing to other Visio file types.

Graphic File Types

On the **Export** screen, you can also choose to save your drawing in one of four graphic file formats. This table describes each format.

Format	Description
Portable Network Graphic (*.png)	A raster graphic format suitable for printing.
JPEG File Interchange Format (*.jpg)	A raster graphic format suitable for a web page.
EMF Enhanced Metafile (*.emf)	A vector graphic suitable for any use in other Windows Office files.
SVG Scalable Vector Graphics (*.svg)	A vector graphic suitable for use on a web page.

Figure 5-12: Exporting a drawing to other graphic file types.

The AutoCAD Drawing Format

On the **Export** screen, you can choose to save your drawing in AutoCAD format. AutoCAD is a software application for 2D and 3D computer-aided design (CAD) and drafting. AutoCAD is used across a range of industries, including architects and engineers.

Figure 5-13: Exporting a drawing to AutoCAD format.

Note: You can learn more about AutoCAD at **http://www.autodesk.com/products/ autodesk-autocad/overview**.

Web Page Publication

On the **Export** screen, you can choose to save your drawing as a web page. When you select this option, Visio creates an HTML home page with the same name as the drawing, as well as a folder containing the graphic and other files needed to render the page. If your Visio drawing contains more than one page, the HTML home page will include links to additional HTML pages for each Visio page. You can then deploy these HTML and support files on your company's website.

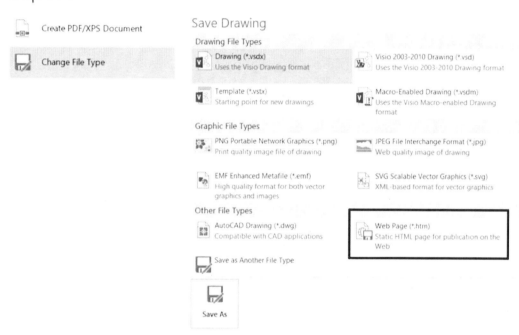

Figure 5-14: Exporting a drawing to a web page.

 Access the Checklist tile on your LogicalCHOICE course screen for reference information and job aids on How to Export Drawings.

ACTIVITY 5–4
Exporting Drawings

Data File
C:\091115Data\Sharing Drawings\EE Territories Map.vsdx

Before You Begin
Visio is open.

Scenario
Gary Thiele, the U.S. and Canada sales manager, was very impressed by the sales territories map you created for him. However, he asked for a few revisions:

- Add a title.
- Add the EE logo.
- Add a confidentiality notice.
- Make Alaska smaller and move it closer to Washington.
- Move Hawaii closer to California.
- Make the contiguous states larger.

After you make these changes, Gary asks you to export the drawing to a PDF so that he can share it with his team by email. None of the sales representatives have a Visio license and some of them work remotely.

1. In Visio, open **C:\091115Data\Sharing Drawings\EE Territories Map**.

Notice that, when the drawing is open, the **External Data** window also opens. If desired, you can close or hide this window.

2. Export the drawing to PDF.

a) On the ribbon, select the **FILE** tab.
b) On the **Backstage**, select **Export**.
c) Verify that **Create PDF/XPS Document** is selected.
d) Select the **Create PDF/XPS** button.

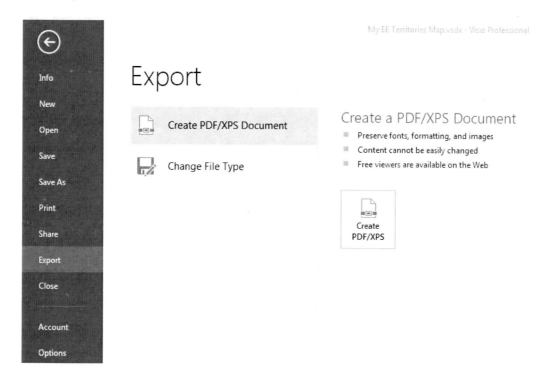

e) In the **Publish as PDF or XPS** dialog box, navigate to the **C:\091115Data\Sharing Drawings** folder.
f) In the **File name** field, change the name to *My EE Territories Map Final.pdf*
g) Review the **Optimize for** setting and select the **Minimum size (publishing online)** radio button.

    Because this PDF will be distributed by email, you want it to be as small as possible.

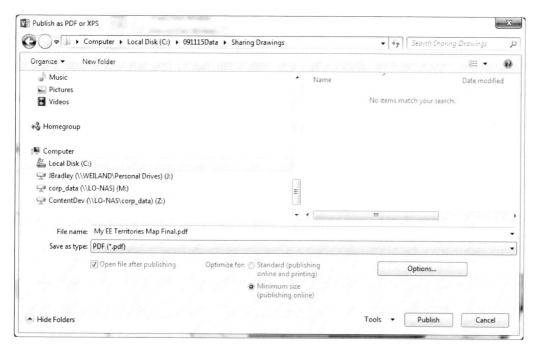

h) Select the **Publish** button.

Visio exports the drawing to PDF. The PDF file opens so that you can review it.

3. Close **My EE Territories Map Final.pdf**.

4. Close **My EE Territories Map Final.vsdx**.

TOPIC E

Print Drawings

Even in this digital age, paper output is often essential and sometimes preferred. This topic shows you how to make sure your drawings look their best in print.

The Print Screen on the Backstage

The **Print** screen on the **Backstage** contains a number of controls that enable you to print your drawing on paper in exactly way you want.

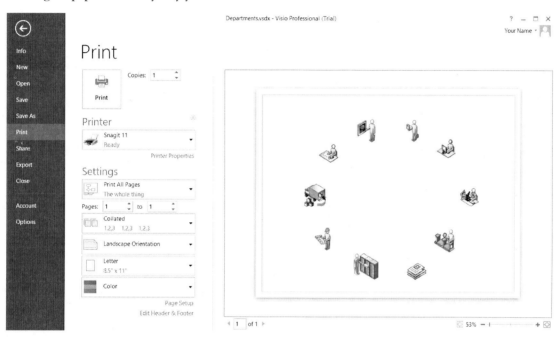

Figure 5-15: The Print screen.

This table describes each setting and command on the **Print** screen.

Control	Use
Print	After you review and change the print settings below, select this button to print.
Copies	Choose how many copies of the page to print.
Printer	Select a printer.
Printer Properties	Edit the properties of the selected printer.

Control	Use
Range	Choose how much of the drawing you want to print. The options are: • **Print All Pages** • **Print Current Page** • **Custom Print** • **Print Selection** • **Current View** If you chose **Custom Print**, use the **Pages** spin boxes to indicate the start and end of the range.
Collation	Choose whether the output should be collated or uncollated.
Orientation	Choose whether the output should be landscape or portrait.
Size	Select the size of the paper.
Color	Choose to print in color or black and white.
Page Set Up	Open the **Page Set Up** dialog box, which will be discussed later in this topic.
Edit Header & Footer	Open the **Header & Footer** dialog box, which will also be discussed later in this topic.
Print Preview	See how your printed page will look. Use the navigation controls at the bottom left to move the preview from one page to another. Use the zoom controls at the bottom right to change the size of the preview.

The Page Setup Dialog Box

If you select the **Page Setup** link on the **Print** screen, the **Page Setup** dialog box opens, displaying a number of additional print options grouped into six tabs.

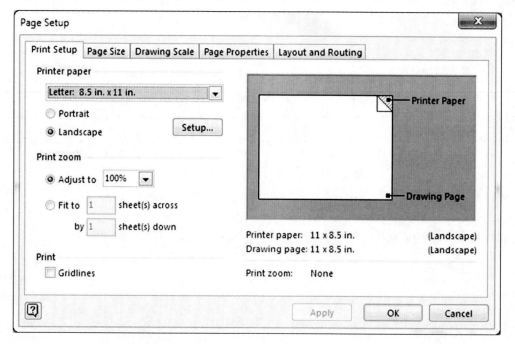

Figure 5-16: The Page Setup dialog box.

The following table describes some of the print options you can use on each tab of the dialog box.

Tab	Use
Print Setup	Make large drawings fit on a printed page or make small drawings larger.
Page Size	Let Visio expand the page as need or constrain Visio to a pre-defined or custom page size.
Drawing Scale	Change the scale of the drawing page to a pre-defined or custom scale. The pre-defined options are **Architectural**, **Civil Engineering**, **Metric**, and **Mechanical Engineering**.
Page Properties	Change the page **Name**, **Background**, and **Measurement units**.
Layout and Routing	Change how Visio handles connectors.

The Edit Header & Footer Dialog Box

If you select the **Edit Header & Footer** link on the **Print** screen, the **Edit Header & Footer** dialog box opens—enabling you to choose the text that will be printed at the top and bottom of the page. For each of the six fields, you can select pre-defined options [such as **File name**, **Current date (short)**, and **Page number**] that appear in the dialog box as codes [such as **&f**, **&d**, and **&p**]. You can also type custom text into each field. This dialog box also enables you to choose the margins and font for your headers and footer.

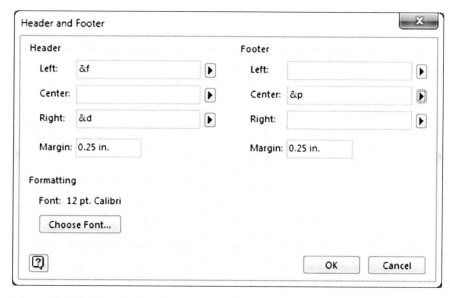

Figure 5-17: The Edit Header & Footer dialog box.

Fastpath: To learn more about Visio, you can access the LearnTO **Identify the Top Five Creative Uses for Visio** presentation from the **LearnTO** tile on the LogicalCHOICE Course screen.

Access the Checklist tile on your LogicalCHOICE course screen for reference information and job aids on How to Print Drawings.

ACTIVITY 5-5
Printing Drawings

Data File

C:\091115Data\Sharing Drawings\EE Order Fulfillment Process Final.vsdx

Before You Begin

Visio is open.

Scenario

Roxana Addison, the vice president of operations, was very happy with the order fulfillment process drawing you created for her. She is meeting with her team tomorrow. She asked you to print 25 color copies of the drawing. However, she wants several items to appear in the header or footer:

* The title of the document
* The current date
* The company name
* A confidentiality notice

---

1. In Visio, open **C:\091115Data\Sharing Drawings\EE Order Fulfillment Process Final.vsdx**.

2. Access the **Print** screen.
   a) On the ribbon, select the **FILE** tab.
   b) On the **Backstage**, select **Print**.

3. Choose a printer.
   a) On the **Print** screen, select the **Printer** drop-down arrow.
   b) Select **Microsoft XPS Document Writer**.

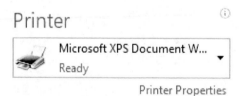

4. Review the **Settings** section.

Settings

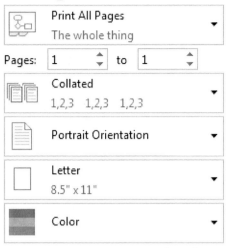

Print All Pages
The whole thing

Pages: 1 to 1

Collated
1,2,3   1,2,3   1,2,3

Portrait Orientation

Letter
8.5" x 11"

Color

Page Setup
Edit Header & Footer

All of the default settings are fine for this document.

5. Edit the header and footer.

   a) Select **Edit Header & Footer**.
   b) In the **Header and Footer** dialog box, in the **Header Left** field, ensure that the **&f** code appears.
   c) In the **Header Right** field, ensure the **&D** code appears.
   d) In the **Footer Left** field, ensure **Emerald Epicure** appears.
   e) In the **Footer Right** field, ensure **CONFIDENTIAL!** appears.

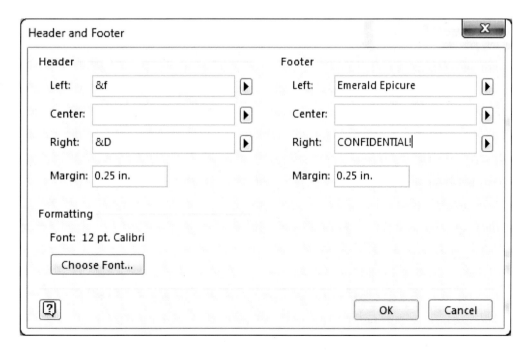

   f) Select **OK** to close the dialog box.

6. On the right side of the **Print** screen, examine the drawing in **Print Preview**.

Notice that some of the text in the header and footer is close to or overlaps some elements of the drawing.

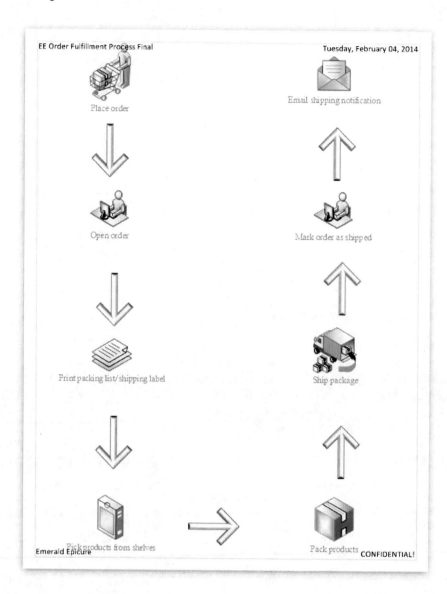

7. Adjust the **Page Setup**.

   a) Select **Page Setup**.

b) In the **Page Setup** dialog box, on the **Print Setup** tab, in the **Print zoom** section, ensure that the **Fit to** radio button is selected. Keep the default of 1 sheet across by 1 sheet down.

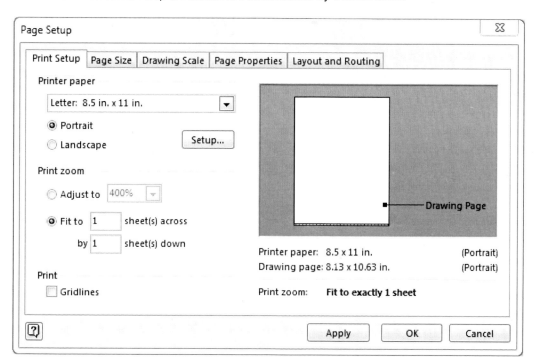

c) Select the **OK** button to apply the change and close the dialog box.

8. Examine the drawing in **Print Preview** again.

The spacing between the headers/footers and drawing elements is better.

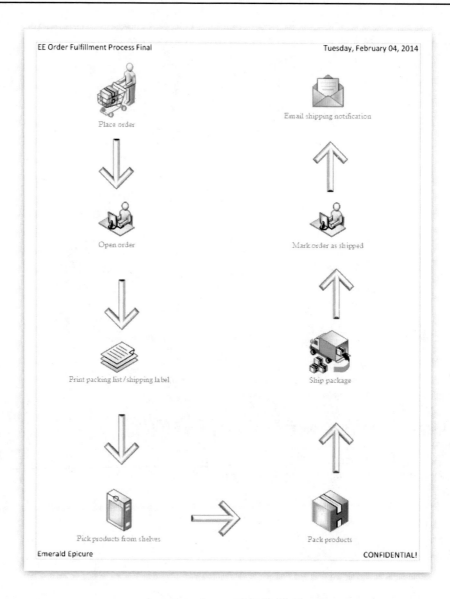

9. Select the **Copies** field and type *25*

10. Select the **Print** button.
    If you had selected a physical printer, your copies would be printed. However, because the Microsoft XPS Document Writer is a printer driver, Visio wants to create an XPS file.

11. In the **Save file as** dialog box, select **Cancel**.

12. In the **Quick Access Toolbar**, select the **Save** icon. 💾

13. Close Visio.

Summary

In this lesson, you became familiar with the many ways you can share Visio drawings with others. You used OneDrive to share drawings with clients and contractors who don't have access to your company's network. You commented on Visio drawings shared by others. You used to methods to insert Visio drawings into other Office files. You exported Visio drawings to other file formats. Finally, you learned to make sure your documents look their best in print.

In your work environment, how will you share draft Visio drawings with colleagues for review and comment?

In what media will your finished Visio drawings be used?

 Note: Check your LogicalCHOICE Course screen for opportunities to interact with your classmates, peers, and the larger LogicalCHOICE online community about the topics covered in this course or other topics you are interested in. From the Course screen you can also access available resources for a more continuous learning experience.

Course Follow-Up

Congratulations! You have completed the Microsoft® Visio® 2013: Part 2 course. In this course, you learned advanced ways of using Visio. Now you are equipped with the knowledge and skills to be a more efficient and effective Visio user.

What's Next?

Depending on your proficiency with Microsoft® Office, you can learn more about the individual applications by checking out the associated Logical Operations courses.

You are also encouraged to explore Visio further by actively participating in any of the social media forums set up by your instructor or training administrator through the **Social Media** tile on the LogicalCHOICE Course screen.

A Using Diagram Standards

Lesson Time: 30 minutes

Lesson Objectives

In this lesson, you will use diagram standards. You will:

- Model business process with a BPMN template.

- Model software architecture with UML templates.

Appendix Introduction

A number of industries have developed formal standards for diagramming. Such standards provide a common visual language that can be used by everyone in the industry. In this lesson, you'll use Visio to build diagrams that comply with two of those standards.

TOPIC A

Model Business Processes

Every company engages in business process. In some situations, existing business process need to be clearly documented so that all employees can follow them consistently. In other situations, new business process must the planned before they are implemented. In this topic, you'll use Visio to build business process diagrams that comply with an internationally recognized BPMN standard.

Business Processes

A *business process* is a set of related, structured activities that produce a specific business result. Examples of business processes include:

- Receiving orders
- Invoicing customers
- Shipping products
- Updating employee information

BPMN

Business Process Model and Notation (BPMN) is a standardized system for graphically representing business processes. BPMN can be readily understood by all business stakeholders, including:

- Analysts who create and refine business processes
- Technical developers who implement business processes
- Business managers who monitor and control business processes

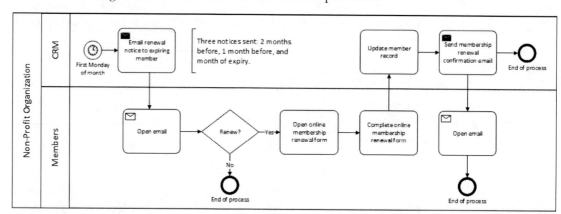

Figure A-1: A business process modeled with BPMN.

Basic Elements of BPMN

The following table describes the basic elements of BPMN.

Basic Elements	Commonly Used Symbols	Notes
Events	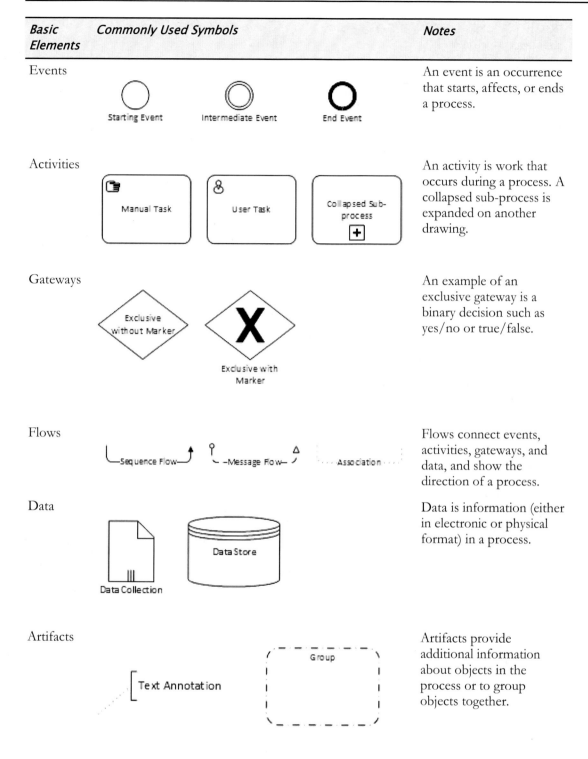	An event is an occurrence that starts, affects, or ends a process.
Activities		An activity is work that occurs during a process. A collapsed sub-process is expanded on another drawing.
Gateways		An example of an exclusive gateway is a binary decision such as yes/no or true/false.
Flows		Flows connect events, activities, gateways, and data, and show the direction of a process.
Data		Data is information (either in electronic or physical format) in a process.
Artifacts		Artifacts provide additional information about objects in the process or to group objects together.

Basic Elements	Commonly Used Symbols	Notes
Swimlanes	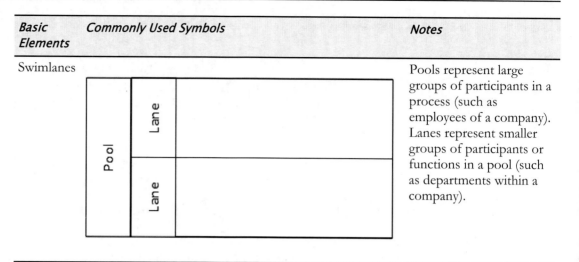	Pools represent large groups of participants in a process (such as employees of a company). Lanes represent smaller groups of participants or functions in a pool (such as departments within a company).

 Note: BPMN standards are maintained by the Object Management Group (OMG). Visit **http://www.bpmn.org** for more information.

The BPMN Diagram Template

Visio includes a **BPMN Diagram** template that you can use to construct business process templates that meet BPMN standards. This template isn't featured on the **Start** screen, so you'll need to search for it online and install it.

Figure A–2: Searching for the BMPN Diagram template from the Start screen.

The **BPMN Diagram** template includes a **BPMN Basic Shapes** stencil. After you add a basic BPMN shape to the drawing, you can use the right-click menu to apply BPMN symbols and other attributes to the shape.

Shapes

‹

STENCILS | SEARCH

More Shapes ▶

Quick Shapes

BPMN Basic Shapes

☐ Task	◇ Gateway
◎ Intermediate Event	◯ End Event
◯ Start Event	⊞ Collapsed Sub-Process
Expanded Sub-Process	Text Annotation
→ Sequence Flow	· · · · Association
○–▷ Message Flow	✉ Message
🗋 Data Object	🗄 Data Store
Group	▭ Pool / Lane

Figure A-3: The BPMN Basic Shapes stencil.

If your BPMN diagram becomes too complex, you can use the **PROCESS→Create from Selection** command to convert some of the steps into a sub-process. Visio will show a collapsed sub-process indicator on the original page and the expanded sub-process on a new, linked page.

You can ensure that your diagram meets BPMN 2.0 specifications by using the **PROCESS→Check Diagram** command. Visio will validate the diagram against BMPM rules and display a list of issues that you should address.

 Access the Checklist tile on your LogicalCHOICE course screen for reference information and job aids on How to Model Business Processes.

ACTIVITY A-1
Modeling Business Processes

Before You Begin

Ensure Visio Professional 2013 is open.

Scenario

Andrew Bowen, vice president of sales at Emerald Epicure, asked you to create a BPMN diagram for a quoting process. Because the process is not currently documented, it is implemented differently by each sales representative. This has resulted in several problems internally and externally. Andrew hopes that a BPMN diagram will help reduce inconsistency and prevent future problems. Here's the process Andrew would like diagrammed:

1. Customer emails request for quote.
2. Sales representative receives quote request.
3. Sales representative manually prepares quote.
4. Sales manager reviews quote.
5. Is the quote okay?

   • If no, continue to step 6.
   • If yes, go to step 7.

6. Sales manager revises quote.
7. Sales manager approves quote.
8. Sales representative emails quote to customer.
9. Customer receives quote.

You want to end up with something like this:

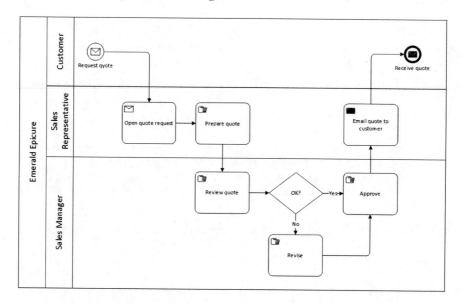

1. Start a new BPMN diagram.
   a) On the ribbon, select the **FILE** tab.
   b) On the **Backstage**, verify that you are viewing the **New** section. If you aren't, select it.

c)   In the **Search for online templates** field, type *BPMN* and select the magnifying glass icon.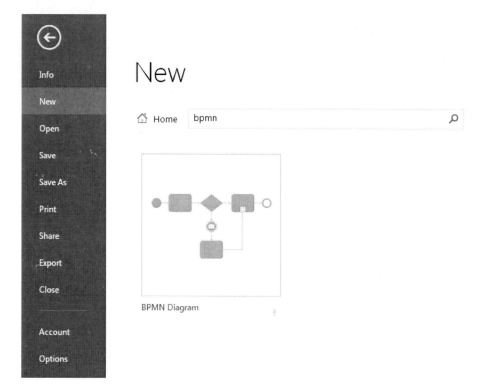

d)   Double-click the **BPMN Diagram** tile.

e) In the **BPMN Diagram** preview, verify that the **US Units** radio button is selected and select **Create**.

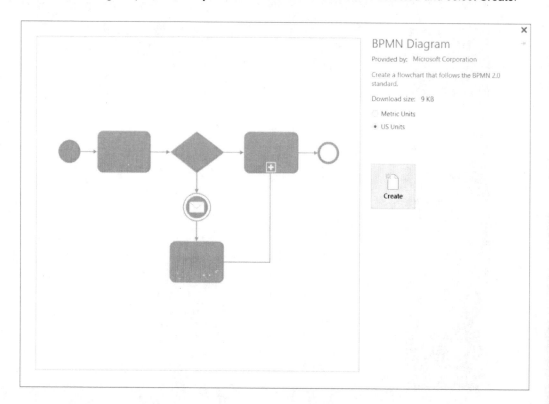

Visio opens a blank drawing page with a **BPMN Diagram** stencil in the **Shapes** window.

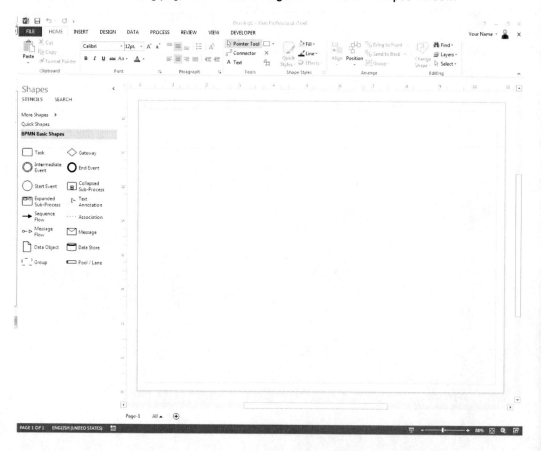

2. Add lane elements to the BPMN diagram.

   a) Drag the **Pool/Lane** shape from the **Shapes** window to the top of the drawing page.
      A swimlane labeled **Function** appears at the top of the drawing page.

   b) For a second time, drag the **Pool/Lane** shape from the **Shapes** window to the drawing page and glue it to the bottom of the first swimlane.
      Visio automatically merges the two swimlanes into a pool labeled **Title**.

   c) For a third time, drag the **Pool/Lane** shape from the **Shapes** window to the drawing page and snap it to the bottom of the second swimlane.
      Visio automatically adds the swimlane to the pool.

Title	Function	
	Function	
	Function	

   d) In the pool, double-click **Title** and change the text to **Emerald Epicure**.

   e) In the first swimlane, double-click **Function** and change the text to **Customer**.

   f) In the second swimlane, double-click **Function** and change the text to **Sales Representative**.

   g) In the third swimlane, double-click **Function** and change the text to **Sales Manager**.

Emerald Epicure	Customer	
	Sales Representative	
	Sales Manager	

3. Add a start event to the BPMN diagram.

   a) Drag the **Start Event** shape from the **Shapes** window to the left end of the **Customer** swimlane.

   b) In the **Customer** swimlane, double-click the event, type *Request quote* and press **Esc**.

c) Right-click the **Request quote** event and, from the shortcut menu, select **Trigger/Result→Message**.

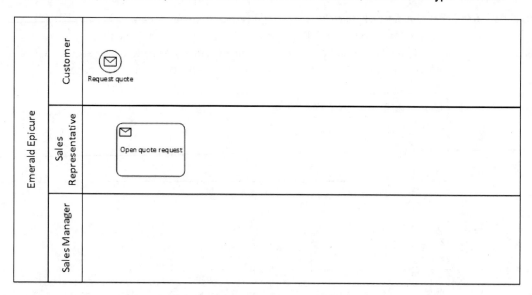

4. Add an activity element to the BPMN diagram.

   a) Drag the **Task** shape from the **Shapes** window to about an inch from left end of the **Sales Representative** swimlane.

   b) In the **Sales Representative** swimlane, double-click the task, type *Open quote request* and press **Esc**.

   c) Right-click the **Open quote request** task and, from the shortcut menu, select **Task Type→Receive**.

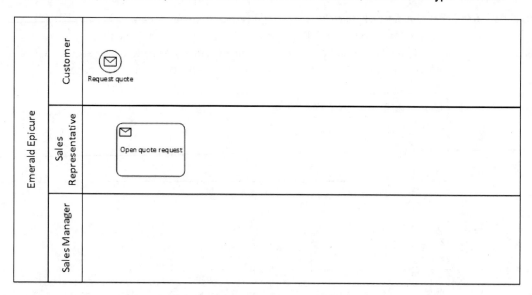

5. Add a flow element to the BPMN diagram.

   a) Drag the **Message Flow** shape from the **Shapes** window to the **Customer** swimlane.

   b) Attach the beginning point of the flow arrow to the right side of the **Request quote** event.

c) Attach the ending point of the flow arrow to the top side of the **Open quote request** task.

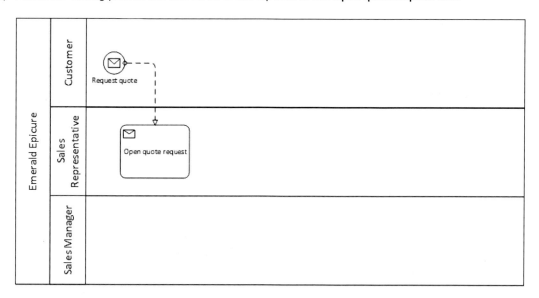

6. Add a second activity element to the BPMN diagram.

   a) Hover the mouse pointer over the **Open quote request** task.
      Notice that **AutoConnect** arrows appear above, below, to the left, and to the right of the **Open quote request** task.

 Note: If you don't see AutoConnect arrows, you may need to enable AutoConnect. On the ribbon, select the **VIEW** tab and, in the **Visual Aids** group, check the **AutoConnect** check box.

   b) Hover the mouse pointer over the right **AutoConnect** arrow.
      Notice that a Quick Shapes mini-tool bar appears.

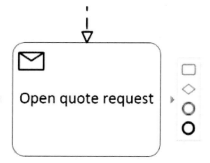

    c) From the **Quick Shapes** mini-toolbar, select the rounded rectangle ⬜ at the top.

       Visio adds a new, blank task to the right of **Open quote request** task and automatically connects the two tasks with a sequence flow object.

    d) Double-click the blank task, type *Prepare quote* and press **Esc**.

    e) Right-click the **Prepare quote** task and, from the shortcut menu, select **Task Type→Manual**.

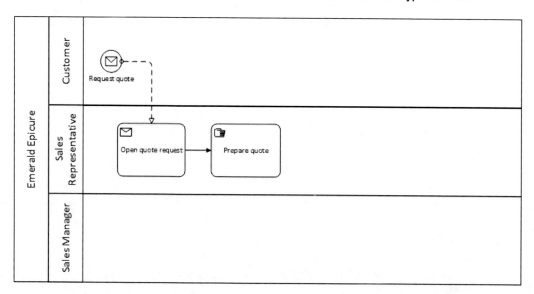

7. Add a third activity element to the BPMN diagram.
    a) Manually add a new task to the **Sales Manager** swimlane, directly below the **Prepare quote** task.
    b) Label the new task *Review quote*
    c) Change the **Task Type** to **Manual**.
    d) Manually add a new sequence flow object between the **Prepare quote** and **Review quote** tasks.

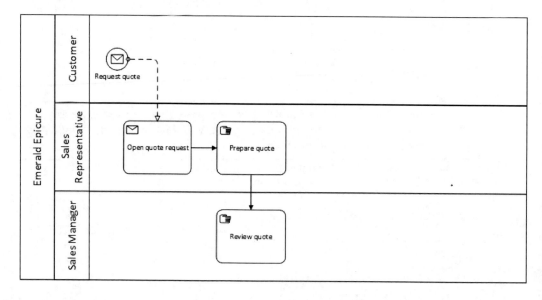

8. Add a gateway object to the BPMN diagram.
    a) If it is selected, deselect **Review quote** tasks.
    b) Hover the mouse pointer over the **Review quote** task.
    c) Hover the mouse pointer over the right **AutoConnect** arrow.
    d) From the **Quick Shapes** mini-toolbar, select the diamond.

Visio adds a new, blank gateway to the right of **Review request** task and automatically connects the task and the gateway with a sequence flow object.

e) Double-click the blank gateway, type *OK?* and press **Esc**.

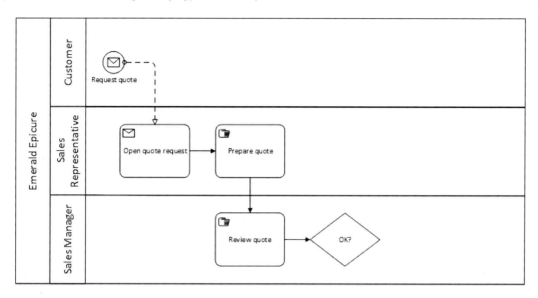

9. Add mutually exclusive paths to the BMPN diagram.

   a) Below the **OK?** gateway object, use AutoConnect to add a task named **Revise**.
      Visio automatically expands the height of the **Sales Manager** swimlane to accommodate the new task.

   b) To the right of the **OK?** gateway object, use AutoConnect to add a task named *Approve*

   c) Double-click the sequence flow object between **OK?** and **Revise**, type *No* and press **Esc**.

   d) Double-click the sequence flow object between **OK?** and **Approve**, type *Yes* and press **Esc**.

   e) For both the **Revise** and **Approve** tasks, change the **Task Type** to **Manual**.

   f) Manually add a sequence flow object between the **Revise** and **Approve** tasks.

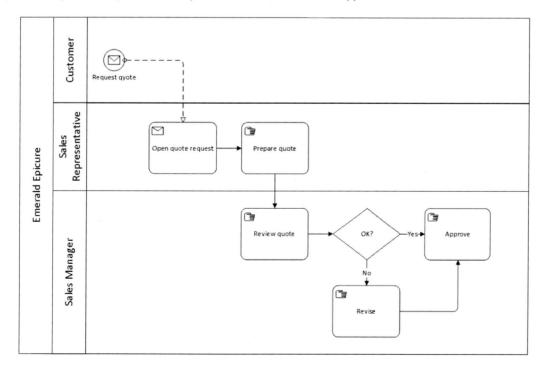

10. Add a final activity element to the BPMN diagram.
    a) Manually add a new task to the **Sales Representative** swimlane, directly above the **Approve** task.
    b) Label the new task *Email quote to customer*
    c) Change the **Task Type** to **Send**.
    d) Manually add a new sequence flow object between the **Approve** and **Email quote to customer** tasks.

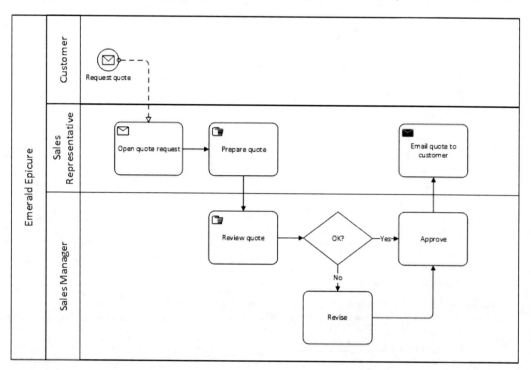

11. Add an end event object to the BPMN diagram.
    a) Drag the **End Event** shape from the **Shapes** window to the left end of the **Customer** swimlane.
    b) In the **Customer** swimlane, double-click the circle, type *Receive quote* and press **Esc**.
    c) Right-click the **Receive quote** event and, from the shortcut menu, select **Trigger/Result→Message**.

d) Manually add a message flow object between the **Email quote to customer** task and the **Receive quote** event.

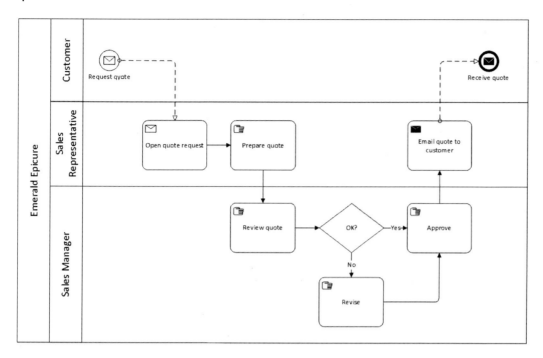

12. Validate the BPMN diagram.

a) On the ribbon, select the **PROCESS** tab.

b) In the **Diagram Validation** group, select the **Check Diagram** command.
Visio opens the Issues window and lists eight issues.

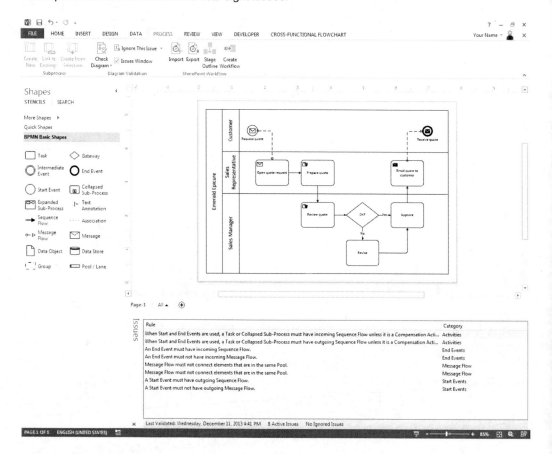

c) Select each issue listed to see which objects are at fault.

All of these issues are a result of incorrectly using the message flow object in two places and can be easily corrected.

d) Right-click a message flow object (represented by dashed arrow) and change the object type from **Message Flow** to **Sequence Flow**. Repeat for the remaining message flow object.

e) Select the **Check Diagram** command again.
This time, Visio finds no validation issues.

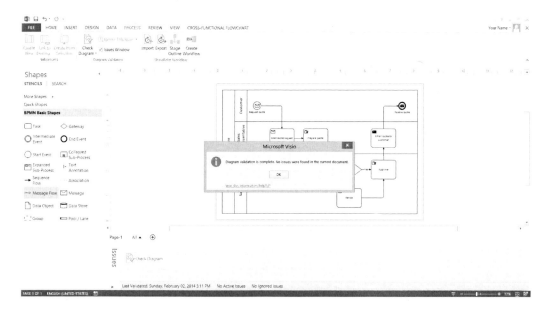

13. Save the BPMN diagram to the **C:\091115Data\Using Diagram Standards** folder as *My Emerald Epicure Quote Process.vsdx*

14. Close the drawing.

TOPIC B

Model Software Architecture

In this digital age, businesses increasingly rely on software solutions. Even if you aren't a programmer, at some point in your career you're likely to be part of a software project. In this topic, you'll use Visio to build software architecture diagrams that comply with the internationally recognized UML standard.

UML

Unified Modeling Language (UML) is a standardized, general-purpose modeling language used by the software engineering field. UML includes a set of graphic notation techniques to create visual models of object-oriented, software-intensive systems.

As shown in this table, UML recognizes 14 types of diagrams grouped into two categories.

Categories	Types
Structure diagrams emphasize what things must be present in the system being modeled. They are used to document the architecture of software systems.	• Class Diagrams • Component Diagrams • Deployment Diagrams • Object Diagrams • Package Diagrams • Profile Diagrams • Composite Structure Diagrams
Behavior diagrams emphasize what must happen in the system being modeled. They are used to describe the functionality of software systems.	• Use Case Diagrams • Activity Diagrams • State Machine Diagrams • Sequence Diagrams • Communication Diagrams • Timing Diagrams • Interaction Overview Diagrams

 Note: UML standards are also maintained by the Object Management Group (OMG). Visit **http://www.uml.org** for more information.

UML Templates

Visio includes six UML templates, each with its own stencil. The templates aren't featured on the **Start** screen, so you'll need to search for them.

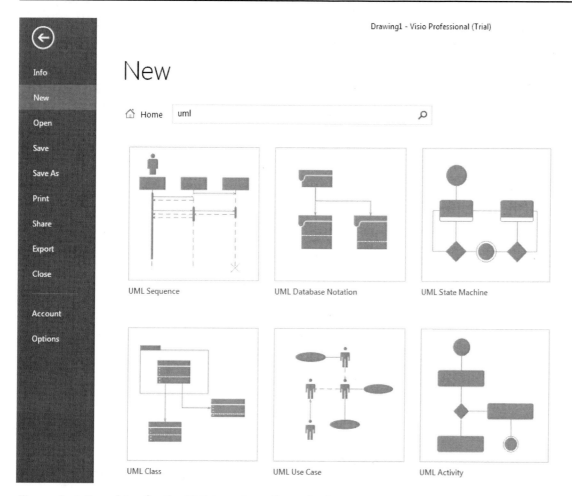

Figure A-4: Searching for the UML templates from the Start screen.

Template	Use	Stencil			
UML State Machine	Describes the behavior of objects that act differently depending to their current state.	◇ Choice		⬛ Composite state	
		◎ Final state		○ Initial state	
		▱ Note		⬛ State	
		⬛ State with internal ...		⬛ Submachine state	

Template	Use	Stencil	
UML Use Case	Depicts the actors involved in a system, different functions needed by those actors, and how these different functions interact.	Actor, Dependency, Generalizati..., Subsystem	Association, Extend, Include, Use Case
UML Sequence	Shows how objects interact with each other, and in what order, for a particular scenario.	Activation, Alternative fragment, Interaction operand, Message, Optional fragment, Return Message	Actor lifeline, Asynchron... Message, Loop fragment, Object lifeline, Other fragment, Self Message
UML Class	Shows the classes in a system, attributes and operations of each class, and the relationship between each class.	Aggregation, Class, Dependency, Enumeration, Interface, Member, Package (collapsed), Separator	Association, Composition, Directed Association, Inheritance, Interface Realization, Note, Package (expanded)

Template	Use	Stencil	
UML Activity	Describes the business or operational workflow of any component in a system.	⬭ Action ◯ Final node ◯ Initial node ◇ Merge Node ▯ Swimlane (vertical)	◇ Decision ▭ Fork node ▭ Join node ⬠ Note
UML Database Notation	This template doesn't correspond to a recognized UML diagram. It is similar to the **UML Class** template. It can be used to diagram a database that is part of a system, providing a look that is consistent with the other UML templates.	--- Attribute ⊢-- Primary Key Attribute ⌐ Relationship	▭ Entity ...... Primary Key Separator

---

Access the Checklist tile on your LogicalCHOICE course screen for reference information and job aids on How to Model Software Architecture.

ACTIVITY A-2
Modeling Software Architecture

Before You Begin
Visio Professional 2013 is open.

Scenario
Emerald Epicure plans to build a web portal (code named Oliver) that will enable customers to order products online. Rob Bowlin, the vice president for information technology at Emerald Epicure, wants you build the UML diagrams that will model this system before it is built. A use case diagram is the first diagram on his list. Here are the use cases that Rob would like diagrammed:

- New customer registers on Oliver
- Existing customer logs in to Oliver
- Existing customer places order on Oliver
- Existing customer pays for order on Oliver
- Fulfillment Team Member (FTM) logs in to Oliver
- FTM generates packing lists and shipping labels from Oliver

---

1. Start a new UML use case diagram.
   a) On the ribbon, select the **FILE** tab.
   b) On the **Backstage**, verify that you are viewing the **New** section. If you aren't, select it.

c) In the **Search for online templates** field, type *UML* and select the magnifying glass icon.

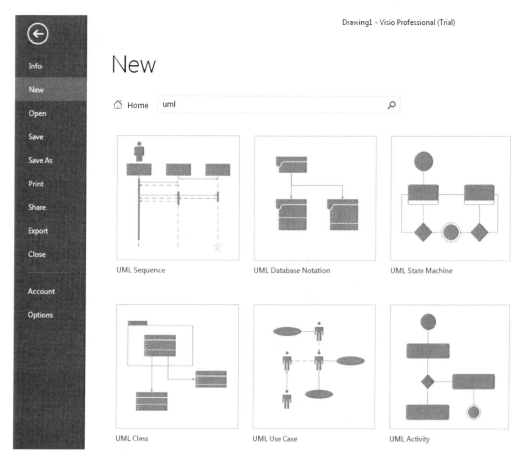

d) Double-click the **UML Use Case** tile.

e) In the **UML Use Case** preview, verify that the **US Units** radio button is selected and select **Create**.

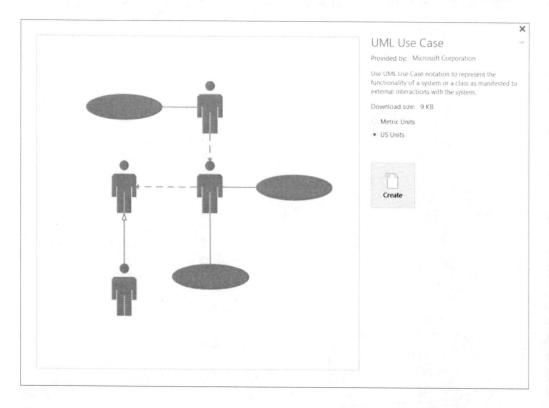

Visio opens a blank drawing page with a **UML Use Case** stencil in the **Shapes** window.

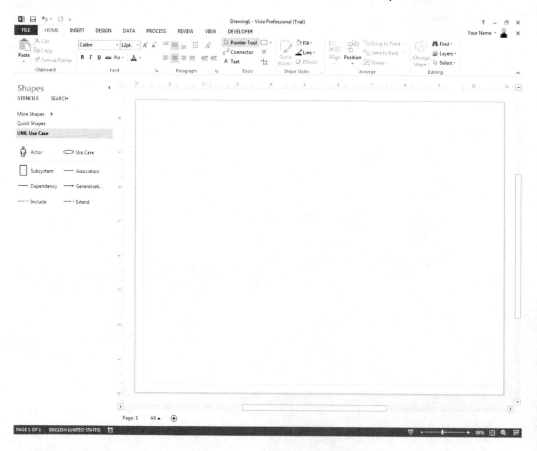

2. Add a system element to the UML use case diagram.
   a) Drag the **Subsystem** shape from the **Shapes** window to the top center of the drawing page.
   b) Double-click **Name**, type *Oliver* and press **Esc**.

3. Add an actor element to the UML use case diagram.
   a) Drag the **Actor** shape from the **Shapes** window to the drawing page. Drop it on the outside left side of the **Oliver** system rectangle.
   b) On the drawing page, double-click the actor element, type *New customer* and press **Esc**.

4. Add a use case element to the UML use case diagram.
   a) Hover the mouse pointer over the **New customer** actor.
   b) Hover the mouse pointer over the right **AutoConnect** arrow.

c) From the **Quick Shapes** mini-toolbar, select the oval.

New customer

Visio adds a new, blank use case in the **Oliver** system and automatically connects the **New customer** actor and the use case object.

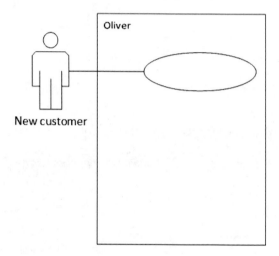

d) Double-click the blank use case, type *Register* and press **Esc**.

e) If desired, reposition the **Register** use case oval so that it is horizontally centered in the **Oliver** system rectangle.

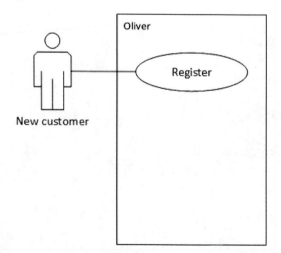

5. Add a second actor element to the UML use case diagram.

a) Drag the **Actor** shape from the **Shapes** window to the drawing page. Drop it below the **New customer** actor.

b) On the drawing page, double-click the new actor element, type *Existing customer* and press **Esc**.

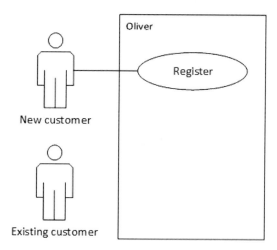

6. Add a second use case element to the UML diagram.
   a) Hover the mouse pointer over the **Existing customer** actor.
   b) Hover the mouse pointer over the right **AutoConnect** arrow.
   c) From the **Quick Shapes** mini-toolbar, select the oval.
      Visio adds a new, blank use case in the Oliver system and automatically connects the Existing customer actor and the use case objects.
   d) Double-click the blank use case, type *Log in* and press **Esc**.
   e) If desired, reposition the **Log in** use case oval so that it is horizontally centered in the **Oliver** system rectangle.

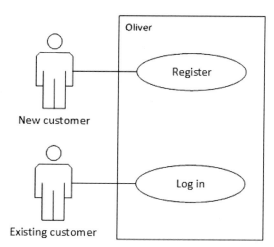

7. Add a third and fourth use case element to the UML diagram.
   a) Increase the length of the **Oliver** system rectangle so that the bottom of the rectangle is near the bottom margin of the drawing page.
   b) Drag the **Use Case** shape from the **Shapes** window to the **Oliver** system rectangle. Drop it below the **Log in** use case.
   c) Double-click the blank use case, type *Place order* and press **Esc**.
   d) Drag the **Use Case** shape from the **Shapes** window to the **Oliver** system rectangle. Drop it below the **Place order** use case.
   e) Double-click the blank use case, type *Pay for order* and press **Esc**.
   f) Drag the **Association** shape from the **Shapes** window to the drawing page. Glue one end to the **Existing customer** actor and the other end to the **Place order** use case.

g) Drag the **Association** shape from the **Shapes** window to the drawing page. Glue one end to the **Existing customer** actor and the other end to the **Pay for order** use case.

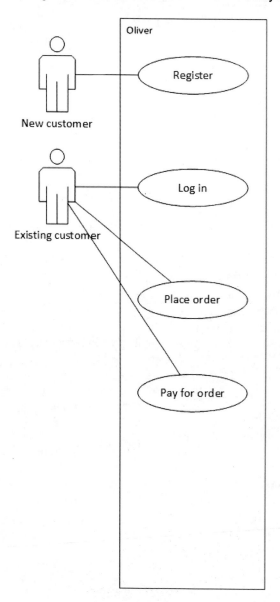

8. Add a third actor element to the UML use case diagram.

a) Drag the **Actor** shape from the **Shapes** window to the drawing page. Drop it on the outside right side of the **Oliver** system rectangle, near the bottom.

b) On the drawing page, double-click the actor element, type *Fulfillment team member* and press **Esc**.

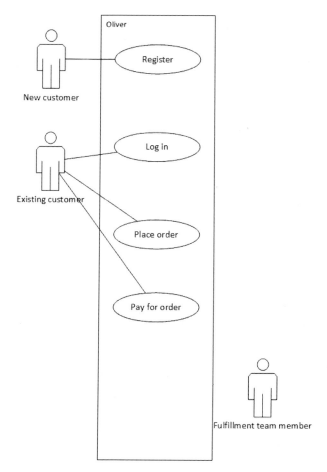

9. Add a fifth use case element to the UML diagram.
   a) Hover the mouse pointer over the **Fulfillment team member** actor.
   b) Hover the mouse pointer over the left **AutoConnect** arrow.
   c) From the **Quick Shapes** mini-toolbar, select the oval.
      Visio adds a new, blank use case in the **Oliver** system and automatically connects the **Fulfillment team member** actor and the use case objects.
   d) Double-click the blank use case, type *Generate packing list* and press **Esc**.

e) If desired, reposition the **Log in** use case oval so that it is horizontally centered in the **Oliver** system rectangle.

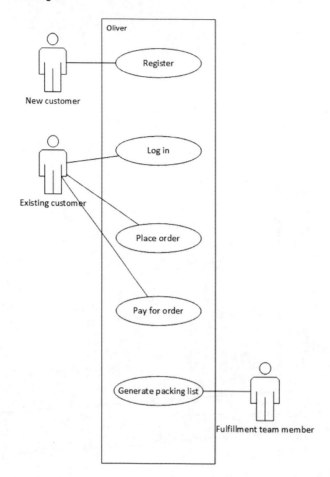

10. Add an **Association** object connecting the **Log in** use case and the **Fulfillment team member** actor.

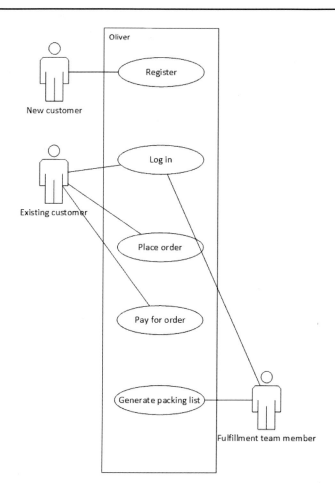

11. If desired, reposition the **Existing customer** and **Fulfillment center employee** actors so that the association lines don't overlap any names or shapes.

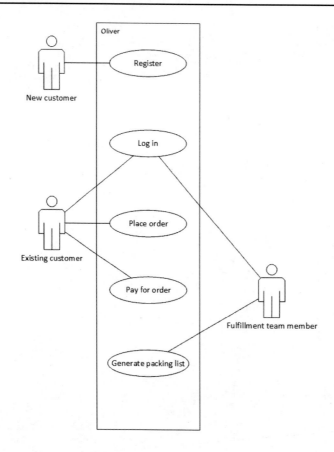

12. Save the UML diagram to the **C:\091115Data\Using Diagram Standards** folder as *My Oliver UML Use Case Diagram.vsdx*

13. Close the drawing.

Summary

In this lesson, you learned how to use Visio to build diagrams that comply with two industry standards—BPMN and UML.

In your company, what business processes might you model with Visio's BPMN template?

- Personnel hiring
- Purchasing
- Accounts payable
- Sales
- Customer service
- Employee termination

In your company, what software architecture might you model with Visio's UML templates?

- Capturing web-to-lead data
- Changing user information
- Resetting a forgotten password
- Linking account and contact records
- Transforming a document from one format to another

 Note: Check your LogicalCHOICE Course screen for opportunities to interact with your classmates, peers, and the larger LogicalCHOICE online community about the topics covered in this course or other topics you are interested in. From the Course screen you can also access available resources for a more continuous learning experience.

Lesson Labs

Lesson labs are provided for certain lessons as additional learning resources for this course. Lesson labs are developed for selected lessons within a course in cases when they seem most instructionally useful as well as technically feasible. In general, labs are supplemental, optional unguided practice and may or may not be performed as part of the classroom activities. Your instructor will consider setup requirements, classroom timing, and instructional needs to determine which labs are appropriate for you to perform, and at what point during the class. If you do not perform the labs in class, your instructor can tell you if you can perform them independently as self-study, and if there are any special setup requirements.

Lesson Lab 1–1
Enhancing the Look of Drawings

Activity Time: 20 minutes

Data File

C:\091115Data\Enhancing the Look of Drawings\PDCA Cycle.vsdx

Scenario

Emerald Epicure is starting a continuous improvement initiative. All employees will be trained to use the Plan-Do-Check-Act (PDCA) process. Arthur Hardison, the CEO of Emerald Epicure, asked you to create a job aid of the PDCA process. You drafted it earlier; now you want to make it more visually attractive.

1. Open Visio, and open **C:\091115Data\Enhancing the Look of Drawings\PDCA Cycle.vsdx**.

2. Apply a theme of your choice to the drawing.

3. Apply a Quick Style of your choice to the **PLAN**, **DO**, **CHECK**, and **ACT** shapes.

4. Manually apply fills, lines, and other effects of your choice to the arrows.

5. Make the **PLAN**, **DO**, **CHECK**, and **ACT** shapes three-dimensional.

6. Add a background to the drawing.

7. Add a border and title to the drawing.

8. Define a custom text style for the explanatory text box next to the **PLAN**, **DO**, **CHECK**, and **ACT** shapes.

9. Apply the custom text style to the text boxes.

10. Save your drawing in **C:\091115Data\Enhancing the Look of Drawings** as *My PDCA Cycle.vsdx*

11. Close the drawing.